WIT AND WISDOM NEEDED IN THE CLASSROOM

A GUIDE FOR TEACHERS

Geneva Fulgham

Rowman & Littlefield Education
Lanham, Maryland • Toronto • Oxford
2006

Published in the United States of America
by Rowman & Littlefield Education
A Division of Rowman & Littlefield Publishers, Inc.
A wholly owned subsidiary of The Rowman & Littlefield Publishing Group, Inc.
4501 Forbes Boulevard, Suite 200, Lanham, Maryland 20706
www.rowmaneducation.com

PO Box 317
Oxford
OX2 9RU, UK

British Library Cataloguing in Publication Information Available

Library of Congress Cataloging-in-Publication Data

Fulgham, Geneva.
  Wit and wisdom needed in the classroom : a guide for teachers /
Geneva Fulgham.
    p. cm.
  ISBN-13: 978-1-57886-434-8 (hardcover : alk. paper)
  ISBN-13: 978-1-57886-435-5 (pbk. : alk. paper)
  ISBN-10: 1-57886-434-8 (hardcover : alk. paper)
  ISBN-10: 1-57886-435-6 (pbk. : alk. paper)
  1. Effective teaching. 2. Classroom management. 3. First year
teachers. I. Title.

LB1025.3.F85 2006
371.102—dc22   2006000391

♾ ™ The paper used in this publication meets the minimum requirements of
American National Standard for Information Sciences—Permanence of Paper
for Printed Library Materials, ANSI/NISO Z39.48-1992.
Manufactured in the United States of America.

CONTENTS

PREFACE

You're going to like teaching. Every teacher I know does. It's enjoyable, giving people information and helping them develop skills they need. It's a genuine thrill to see a face light up and hear someone say, "*Oh, I see!*" and to know that dawn of comprehension is your work.

What you won't like is almost everything else that goes with teaching: in short, the teaching situation. Those of us who have been at it for 29 years or so tend to look back decades ago and think the 1960s were a wonderful time for teachers. Some of that nostalgia is just the usual romanticizing of the past, but it is true that there have been mighty changes in education in the last years of the 20th century.

Not all the changes have been bad, of course, but I do find a lower morale among the teachers I know now than there used to be. I'm going to mention some of these modern distresses because they affect every teacher, but *Wit and Wisdom Needed in the Classroom* is not about what's wrong with teaching. Instead, this book is meant to help you teach more effectively in today's circumstances.

Years passed after I graduated from college before I started teaching, but when I did begin, I said the same thing I hear new teachers say today: "Why didn't they teach me *this* in those education classes, instead of all that theorizing they made us do? Why didn't they tell me how it really is? *Why didn't they teach me to teach?*"

It can be argued that teaching, like writing, has to be learned by doing. Yes and no. Any teacher will tell you that much teaching experience can be passed along by telling and explaining. Through my working years many good teachers told and explained to me many things that could have and should have been taught in education courses. Instead, I learned to teach where most people still do—in the classroom and in the teachers' lounge.

Nobody is too smart to teach. Teaching can take all the wit and wisdom you have, even if you're a genius. It can take all the energy you have, even if you're a living whirlwind. It can take all the patience and compassion you have, even if you're a saint. It's a quality occupation. It is easy to lose sight of this fact when you get bogged down in the snowstorm of paperwork and in the disagreeable details that go with the job. We need to stop and remind ourselves once in a while that *this job is worth doing.*

STARTING FROM SQUARE ONE

SPEAKING OF PRONOUNS

In a book like this, personal pronouns tend to get out of hand. There is the ubiquitous "I," for example, popping up as I mention my work habits or relate some of the things that have happened in my classroom. Please accept it. I have tried to be objective and resort to the third person, but that seemed more awkward in most cases.

The "you" of this book is the teacher who I hope is reading it. I hope parents, too, will want to know what teaching is really like, but I thought they wouldn't mind being silent witnesses to a teacher-to-teacher dialogue. Of course, I didn't allow my students to get away with using an indefinite "you" in their essays, but that's a matter of making sure they learned the rules before they learned when and how to break them. Most modern writing uses the indefinite you in an easy, informal style. I hope my directly addressing the teacher turns out to be comfortable for both of us.

Though I regularly taught students to use he, him, and his when the antecedent might be either male or female, I have elected in this writing to use she, hers, and her. It seems to me only right that a female pronoun should be applied in speaking of a prototype teacher, since the vast majority of public school teachers in this country are female. If male teachers find this offensive, I apologize. I can only say that the female pronouns I have chosen should offend a far smaller number than the less appropriate male pronouns would.

DAY 1

Anything can happen on the day the students come back to school in the fall. Some error in scheduling may cause 80 or 90 students to swarm into your room at one period. Maybe 3 people will show up for the next class. You may have students appear during your "off" period. Bells tend to ring erratically. The loudspeaker often interrupts with announcements that sound hectic if not harassed.

The computer has smoothed out some of our school-opening tangles, but it is still a wild day. A new teacher needs to keep the main objectives in sight and to roll with the punches. Most important of all is sending in a blue card (it's blue in my district) that shows how many students showed up for homeroom and in each class. The counselors use these numbers to level class sizes. It's dirty pool to fake the numbers to make your class enrollment look big so they won't add more students. If you do it, I hope you get caught.

It's best to plan not to speak to any counselor for at least the first week. Counselors' work comes in large lumps, most of it at the opening and closing of each semester. They tend to be grouchy and increasingly uncivil at such times. Leave them alone for a while, and don't let your homeroom kids go near them. Every kid who finds a mistake in his schedule wants to rush to the counselor and get it fixed the first day. Their homeroom teachers need to convince the kids to put the mistake in writing and let the counselors do it their way.

Dive into paperwork as soon as your homeroom assembles. There will be more cards and forms to fill out than you and the students can do, although homeroom will probably be extended. In most schools, homeroom is usually only the first 10 minutes of the day. Enforce quiet when the announcements come on the speaker. There will be some information that is vital to hear. Let your homeroom people know early and often that they must sit in alphabetical order. This is essential for your record keeping, and 10 minutes a day won't kill them.

You can probably get some alphabetizing of homeroom papers done during the passing time before you meet your first period class. Use it.

I had students in each class fill out a small white class card, putting their schedules on the back. I'd record the student's textbook number on that card in a day or two when I issued books. In the meantime, I alphabetized each set of class cards, a tremendous help before I'd had a chance to learn their names.

It is good to have basic information such as the class level and your name on the board that first day. Almost always a student shows up in the wrong room or the wrong level. If it's on the board, he doesn't have to wait around to identify you and your subject before he departs for wherever he belongs.

If you devote the first day to a general introduction of yourself and your course, you have less backtracking to do later. Leveling classes will probably shuffle students in or out of your room during the first week. For the same reason, it's wiser not to issue books the first day or two. It is better to use class sets you can hand out and take up daily, if you simply must use books at all the first day.

Remember, these are perfect strangers to whom you're handing out books. Make sure to count each period so that one book doesn't walk out the door with some student who prefers having an extra at home. One May, a kid with a guilty conscience popped up at the last minute and handed me not only the book I had him charged for, but also one he had "acquired" early in the year. He was just in time to keep me from turning up one book short and having to pay for it.

Since my retirement, our school district has changed textbook distribution over to a system where the teacher is not involved. It's up to each student to get and keep track of the books each class requires. To me, that sounds like dying and going to heaven for all teachers. I really regret never having experienced the new way.

We English teachers like to get a piece of writing from the kids right away for diagnostic purposes. I did that whichever day I issued books. It kept the class gainfully occupied while one student at a time came to my desk and wrote his book number on a master card. Day 1 is a bit too soon for this. Class times vary the first day, too. You need to keep it simple and general.

PLANNING LESSONS

This section is not to be confused with the one labeled "Lesson Plans." This one deals with the thinking that underlies your choices of time and subject matter for a given day or week or grading period. The other one is your show-and-tell for administrators.

In most schools there will be curriculum guides of some sort. They let you know what you are expected to teach and, usually, in what order you are expected to teach it. Some free spirits love to mix up their presentations and teach some things in the fall that are scheduled for the spring and vice versa.

Winging it your way may not get you into trouble with your school administration, but it will certainly make you unpopular with fellow teachers who may have to receive a kid for spring semester to whom you've already taught some of the spring units of work, and who has not had the required fall units. Also, where there are departmental finals, you'll find that mixing spring and fall subject matter probably means you've left out some things that will show up on the midterm exam. That's not fair to the kids.

One way of cheating on the departmental final is (in the privacy of your room) to write on the board during the final: "Omit sections 3, 7, and 10." That gets you off the hook with the kids, but it throws the balance of the exam off kilter. Again, not fair. There's really no substitute for teaching what you are supposed to.

What the curriculum guide can only guess at is how much time you'll need for a given unit of study. You won't know yourself if you haven't taught that course before. Back to the teachers' lounge! Your first step should be to get some ballpark guesses about timing from two or three teachers who are familiar with the material.

Make your lesson plans for 2 weeks if that looks like the right amount of time. Then if it takes you 2 1/2 weeks to get through a certain unit, adjust the plans. Next time you'll know. Nobody I know stays right on the dot of the formal plans, anyway. It isn't possible. You'll find a time and a way to catch up with yourself. Maybe just one class falls behind because of an overlong assembly or a fire drill or some such thing. Bide your time till you see a way to pull that class back into line.

It's important to keep your classes close enough to each other so you can make only one plan for all classes that are on the same level. Sometimes you will have a class that just works more slowly than the others. You'll need to cut out some of the frills and fancy touches with those kids. Trim class discussions. Do what you have to do, but try to bring them within shouting distance of your plan.

No matter what you've written on your plans, try to vary your treatment of the subject matter from class to class. It's good mental exercise for you, and it keeps your presentation from flattening out during the day. If you begin to bore yourself, imagine what the kids are thinking about you! Besides, a joke that brought the house down at second period may wither and die in sixth. If it was good enough, the kids have probably told it to each other at lunch, anyway.

No two classes are at exactly the same intellectual level. You may have a very bright third-period group and a very dull fourth period, both labeled *regular*. Two basic classes or two honors classes can vary just as sharply. You don't have to search for the class level. As days go by, it permeates your consciousness.

For one group, you need to add extra background, invent more questions, keep them busy. For another, you have to water down the material, go slower, avoid asking them anything that isn't in front of their noses. All those adjustments can and should be made by you while you're keeping all five classes within the purview of one written lesson plan. Remember, this flexibility is why you haven't been replaced—yet—by a robot.

If you're in a school situation where you have no curriculum guide, for goodness' sake, sit down with others who are teaching the same subject and grade level and come up with some guidelines you can all agree on. In every school I know about, a certain amount of shuffling of kids from one class to another is bound to go on at the beginning of each semester. You and the other teachers need to be doing approximately the same thing for at least the first week or two so the shuffled kids won't be completely lost as to what's going on.

It's a good general rule to plan more for a day than you can accomplish. If the leftover activity is vital, it can be fitted into the following day. That's a lot better than running out of things to do with

7 or 8 minutes left in the period. However, in case you do someday find yourself in that situation, have a few topics in mind that you can talk about for a short time. I was always reading some book or other and could give my students a report on that.

One of the great disadvantages of teaching public school is that you can never be "right" for all 30 kids in the room. If you're reaching the most intelligent students in the class, you're likely to be going over the heads of the least intelligent. If you lower your sights to include the slowest students, you're boring the higher mentalities to death.

My policy always has been to aim for the middle. That's where most of the kids are. If we go too fast or too far for the lowest mental level of kids, they can come for extra help. We can make it as simple as they need to have it when we have a one-on-one situation.

You should try very hard to make each day different from the last, even though you may be covering one long unit of work. If you went down rows doing an exercise one day, and you think it's vital to do another exercise the next day, at least vary your approach by skipping around the room to call on students during the second session.

Kids love to work at the board. Give them the opportunity every now and then, even if it slows down the lesson. Vocabulary words need to be on the board, anyway, to show the pronunciation. Let the kids do it.

LOUNGE LEARNING

A teacher learns to teach in the lounge. Any experienced teacher will tell you so. Even after 20-plus years of teaching, if a communication that was not clear to me turned up in my box, I went to the lounge and asked whatever teachers were handy for an interpretation. A teacher who is new to a school can always get help there. Sympathy and consolation are also available for whoever needs them.

I must add that spending too much time in the lounge is stultifying and dangerously habit-forming, especially for teachers who smoke. Smokers are usually limited to one lounge, with another designated for nonsmokers. (Nowadays, many schools outlaw smoking altogether, which is tough on those with strong smoking habits. Some of them resort to the restrooms or to their cars in the parking lot when they feel desperate.)

Being a regular in the lounge is dulling because one sees the same few other teachers daily at the same hour. Pretty soon the new wears off each one for the other loungers; conversation languishes, personal details pall. There are only a few remedies for acute boredom under those circumstances: eating, drinking coffee, playing cards.

No matter how many papers a teacher lugs along to grade, her chances of getting work done in the lounge are much smaller than they would be if she were alone in her room. There's always some friend close by who is not grading. In common courtesy, the friend must be noticed, at least now and then.

To any new teacher, or to any old teacher new to the building, my advice is the same. For at least the first year, keep your mouth shut and your ears open when you're in the lounge. You can learn everything from handy teaching tips to personal politics just by listening. You'd do well not to make friends too fast. Listen first and avoid getting deeply involved with chronic bores or others with serious personality deficits. In a faculty situation, it is harder to undo wrong connections than to make them.

Chronic bores expose themselves fast. They're the ones who endlessly relate self-serving anecdotes peppered with clauses like "and I told that kid . . . ," "So I said to that mama . . . ," "then I said, 'Listen, Daddy, your kid needs . . . ,'"—as if any of those conversations were news to experienced teachers. Sometimes you can turn off one of these spouters by becoming absorbed in your paperwork. If that gambit doesn't restore quiet, two alternatives remain: outshout the anecdotal one or leave the area. If you get caught in the same situation more than once or twice, it's *your* fault.

A new teacher shouldn't be afraid to ask about teaching techniques. We all have our treasured ploys, our ways of presenting tedious material to make it more interesting, our means of coaxing the slower students into catching on. Any teacher worth knowing will be happy to share her bag of tricks with somebody else. After all, it's one more opportunity to teach, isn't it?

A beginner who expects to find stimulating academic discussions going on in the lounge is in for 95% disillusionment. For at least that percentage of time, most teachers spend their "off" time talking about the same things that resting people talk about anywhere else. Families, recipes, entertainment, sports, and local gossip make up most of the conversations.

Contrary to what most students suspect, very little lounge time is spent discussing students' possession of or lack of merits. However, it is a good idea for a teacher who is having chronic difficulty with a student to check with his other teachers. Sometimes there really is a personality conflict that can be solved by transferring the kid to another class. Most of the time, queries will uncover the fact that that kid is having trouble in most, if not all, of his other classes, too.

I don't recommend that a teacher start out the year by consulting teachers who have had her students in the past. Kids change a lot from year to year. A nasty little troublemaker in ninth grade can become a real sweetie by his senior year. A teacher needs to give the kid room to change by not getting preconceived ideas about him too early in the year. If a kid who started out in lower grades being a troublemaker still is one at your level, you'll find it out soon enough.

TEACHING IS HARD

Recently a science teacher who had left the classroom years before to work for an oil company visited me. With the oil business in a slump, she was returning to teaching. She told me what it felt like when she first started working a 5-day week, nine to five, for the oil company. "I kept thinking as I worked through the day, 'You people don't know what work *is!*' I'd go home at night and still have energy to do things with my little girl. I could never do that when I taught."

For the first 15 years after college, I did other work: country newspaper editor, radio continuity writer, bank secretary, legal secretary. When I began teaching, I had the same reaction as my friend. Teaching is the hardest work I've ever done. It's exhausting. One does more work in the 9 1/2 months of school than most office workers do in 11 1/2 months.

There is a movement afoot to run schools around the year, staggering semesters so that the buildings will be in continuous use. Pilot programs already exist. I hope it never happens to all our public schools. The chances are just too good that 9-month teachers would be pressured into becoming 12-month teachers, especially as long as low teaching salaries result in chronic teacher shortages. There's a good deal of teacher burnout going on now. There would be a great deal more if teachers had to keep up the school term's exhausting pace all year around.

LEARNING NAMES

To a brand-new teacher, few things are more frightening than the realization that she has 150 new people to cope with, none of whose names she knows. And that isn't counting homeroom!

It takes weeks to "learn" every student to the point where you can greet him or her by name in the hall. Before that time arrives, you will have learned their names sufficiently to remember them when those students are seated in their usual places at the proper period. Before that time arrives, you will, I hope, have made a seating chart for each class.

It helps a little, but not much, to have kids sit in alphabetical order. In recent years I gave up doing that because the kids hate to be alphabetized, and with reason. Imagine day after day, class after class, year after year, having to sit next to some dull, disagreeable person just because your names are close together in the alphabet.

In homeroom, however, I did insist that kids sit in alphabetical order. There are just too many forms that have to be filled out and turned in alphabetized and too many standardized tests that have to be distributed and taken up alphabetically, sometimes right after homeroom period. I figured for only 10 minutes a day or less, the kids can stand to be in order for my convenience.

What I did as soon as my classes settled down (for new teachers, that means as soon as students stop being shifted from one class to another in order to balance teaching loads or to correct programming mistakes) was to make a seating chart for each class, writing in the kids' names in pencil. With that in front of me, I could call on students by name even the first week of school. It's great to see their faces light up when you start knowing who they are.

Penciling the names on the seating chart is the only way. The day before I was going to do that, I used to warn the kids to "be sure you sit tomorrow where you want to stay, because I'll be making a seating chart." Of course, when you find that John and Sue mustn't be allowed to sit together or that Pete and Bill start a fight every other day, you just erase and replace. I usually gave chronic talkers a few days—and a good many warnings—to simmer down. If they couldn't or wouldn't control their talking, I moved them, usually up to the front of the room.

A seating chart is a good place to put other information, too. Sometimes I marked very good or very bad readers with some simple code, or maybe I jotted down the homeroom teacher's name in case the kid was a chronic absentee and I kept having to know who his homeroom teacher was. One can code conduct cuts that way, too, to save cluttering up the grade book. When enough cuts are accumulated, you have justification for the G or P on the report card.

I thought I'd never forget the names of my first year's students. They did really stay in my mind for years. I learned, as time went by, that you retain the names of the kids whom you've just taught until the following September. Then, when the new names go into your memory, the old ones get erased. At least, that's how it worked with me. Of course, you do remember a few names of outstanding kids— good or bad—for years.

Toward the end of the school year, I sometimes explained to my kids that if they came back to see me, they mustn't be offended if I remembered their faces but not their names. I told them their names got erased by the new batch just the way a tape-recorded message does, but their faces stayed with me much longer. That's the truth, and returnees warned didn't seem to mind if I had to ask their names. I might try to get by with "Hello, honey" for brief encounters, but there's no point in faking it past the comfortable point. They can tell if you're glad to see them or not.

When my son came home from school his third or fourth day in first grade, he said, "Why is it that the teacher calls the other kids by both their names, like, 'Bobby Brown' and 'Sally Jones' but when she gets to me, she just calls me 'Joel'?"

I didn't know whether to laugh or cry. You don't teach long before you notice whose names you learn first. They aren't usually the kids who are going to get conduct prizes. Of course, some students just *are* more memorable than others. I think I told him something to that effect.

PHILOSOPHY OF TEACHING

Pretty green eyes sparkling, the new young blonde English teacher smiled around at the rest of us in the lounge. It was the second day of the fall semester. "They're *darling*," she exclaimed, "so interested! I can see they haven't been taught much, but these ninth graders want to learn. All they need is someone to take a real interest in them."

Nobody said, "*We* know," but the thought was going through our minds. Of course, she didn't realize the double insult she'd just handed each of us who had had those kids before. "Haven't been taught much" and "someone to take a real interest" were conclusions she had drawn from what the kids had told her. We knew it wouldn't be long before she began to find out something different.

No English student on any level will admit to having been taught verb tense and pronoun case. Very few will admit to an acquaintance with verbals. As for dependent clauses—! I used to begin each fall shaking my head over the incompetent teachers these kids had had all the way up to me. Gradually I discovered that the next teacher after me heard the same news. Students I had slaved over, grammatically speaking, for 9 months, arrived at the next grade level claiming they'd never heard of grammar.

The same thing holds true in math, science, and social studies. It's just more noticeable, perhaps, in English, since it is admittedly a build-on subject. What I found worked best was to proceed on the assumption that kids do know those elements they were supposed to have learned previously, say, for example, the parts of speech. If a few of them really demonstrate ignorance, they can be coached up to grade level separately. That way, the ones who haven't learned because they have no intention of learning won't be holding back the whole class, and the ones who simply forgot over summer will remember as the class goes forward.

Our pretty blonde began her school career with several dangerous errors of judgment. Taking the kids too literally, she started further back with grammar than she should have for her grade level. The majority of her students, knowing the material already, quickly became bored and restless. She was encountering conduct problems before the first week ended.

Attractive young teachers of both sexes have difficulty realizing that to high school kids their physical attractions will very likely appear dated, especially their clothes and hairstyles. Worse, they certainly don't look *young* to students to whom anyone over 25 is middle-aged!

What misled our young teacher was the intense interest with which the students looked her over the first day. One day in the lounge a teacher was talking about his education professor in graduate school: ". . . makes me so damn mad, always yapping how he wishes he could walk into our classrooms and fascinate our kids with his wonderful teaching techniques. He was telling us last night, 'Why, I could have your kids spellbound inside of 20 minutes.' Of course he could! A *snake*'d fascinate 'em the first day!"

Exactly. The first day you're something new and different. The kids check you over the same as dogs and cats would check a stranger. The trick of the year is, not to catch their interest the first day, but to retain it for the other 179 days.

Another error was our new teacher's belief that she was the only teacher who really cared about the kids. It may not be fashionable to say so in the lounge, but I believe the vast majority of teachers do really care about the students they teach. It seems to me that there is much more dedication and genuine concern in teachers than in any other professional group, including those who earn four or five times as much for their services—and what other profession doesn't earn more?

Our beginner's third false premise was that she could, by caring enough and working hard enough, solve every student's problems and make every student pass. What she didn't know is that in almost every class there is someone who is failing because he (or she) wants to. Unconscious though his motive may be, that kid is going to fail, no matter what the teacher does.

Sometimes a kid just keeps on failing out of sheer, rock-bottom laziness. If he passes, what'll happen? They'll just expect him to do the next thing. Better keep on failing, less strenuous that way.

Sometimes he's failing to spite or get revenge on a parent. Sometimes he's proving something to himself or his folks ("I *can't* do algebra, just as I told you" or "Not making the team ruined my life, so I can't pass biology"). Sometimes the kid has a specific personal goal: to get out of a certain class or to get into a certain class, to "be like" a friend who failed, even to have to repeat a year in order to continue with a favorite sport or elective.

A student I remember was a beautiful brunette. She was so gifted that almost every paper she handed in received a 100 or an A-plus. When she decided to fail, she really didn't know how. She managed it by simply not producing at all. No homework, blank test papers, no book report. I was shocked, and more so when her mother explained that this was what Debbie did from time to time "when she's mad at me."

If I have 10 failures during a grading period, probably not more than 2 or 3 of those kids had to fail for lack of intelligence or background (for example, the foreign student who still has too much of a language barrier). The other 7 or 8 fail for some of the reasons already given here or from other causes such as negative peer pressure, drug abuse, or apathy.

There are students who fail in order to preserve their images. "I'm the guy who never does homework" or "Can you believe that guy? Teacher tells him he's got five zeroes and he never bats an eye!"

After days or weeks of slouching into class tardy and without book, paper, or pens, such a character finds himself in a rut. It would look "uncool" to start carrying materials to class now. He'd literally rather fail than be ridiculed for suddenly reforming.

Drug abusers frequently fail because there is no room in their lives or in their scrambled brains for orderly, coherent thought and work. They seldom make trouble in the classrooms where they are going down for the third time. Their sole objective is to sink quietly, without a trace. There is so much more to be said about drug abuse that I have given it a separate heading elsewhere in this book.

True apathy, I believe, is a result of emotional damage the student has sustained earlier in his life. Frustrated by the blank, uninterested facade this kind of student presents, a teacher often is tempted to badger, hound, bully the kid—anything to strike a spark of interest. Those tactics won't work. Usually, such an emotionally scarred child has buried his feelings so deep that he couldn't respond if he wanted to, and he has learned not to want to.

Divorce is not the only cause of such apathy, but the apathetic kid often does live in a one-parent situation. Any kind of deep or sustained psychological abuse can produce an apathetic child. Sometimes, I am afraid, that emotional damage is done at school by misguided teachers. Wherever the injury comes from, a child you can't reach after you have tried a long time is a child worth mentioning to the counselor. Too often, that counselor is so tied up in paperwork that he or she never gets to know the quiet kids, the ones who don't make waves. Most counselors appreciate being asked to help.

What happened to Angela, the pretty young English teacher? She was a real worker. She was determined to have her 150 students write themes every week. She also believed that each homework assignment deserved a grade. She lugged home enormous stacks of papers daily. She graded early and late and during her 30-minute lunch break. In 2 weeks she was tired; in 2 months she was exhausted, her husband's patience was at breaking point, and her classes were in daily uproar.

It's a shame to see an eager, energetic young woman turn sour and cynical in a semester, but that's what happened. From being sure her students were bright young angels suffering from the ignorance and laziness of us old tabbies, she became convinced that all adolescents are worthless sneaks, liars, and cheats on their way to becoming hardened criminals.

I've always hoped that Angela later became better adjusted and developed more moderate attitudes toward kids and teaching. I don't know. We heard that she was divorced. She moved out of town, and none of us heard from her after that first year.

My first principal, a top-notch one, threw me a curve at our first interview. She asked me to state my philosophy of teaching. I have no memory of what I said. I'd never thought of it before. She's gone to her heavenly reward some years ago—teachers get in free, of course. No exams required for them! Boy, could I give her an earful now!

TEXTBOOKS

In every school where I taught, the teacher was financially responsible for every book she ordered from the bookroom. There is a better way to distribute textbooks. Too late for me, my school district found it. Following are a few cardinal rules to prevent serious erosion of a teacher's final paycheck each May until all schools discover that teachers can and should be left out of the book distribution process.

Usually, books are carried from the bookroom to one's classroom by students. Two Book Requisition cards are filled out by the teacher, showing the number of books ordered. The bookroom manager, usually a teacher or an assistant principal, writes the number of books he is sending and sends one card back to the teacher, keeping the other for office records.

In some schools, one orders all the needed books at one time. For five classes of 30 students each, I would need 150 each of grammars and literatures, for example. (That is, assuming I planned to use the grammars. I didn't always. Sometimes we used workbooks instead.) Of course, a teacher should order a few extra books, since class numbers are not fixed for the first week or so. In other schools, the teacher orders books for each class as she meets that class.

A must: *Count the books the minute they arrive in your room.* "Later" is too late to convince anyone that a counting mistake was made by the book room at the outset. Any discrepancy should be reported immediately. It is best to issue textbooks as soon after they arrive as possible. Piled-up books along the walls are easy prey for students who like to spare themselves the trouble of taking a book home when it's needed, by filching an extra from you.

It is important to plan some assignment that will have students working individually and quietly during textbook distribution. I used a big, stiff Textbook Distribution card. I called each student up in alphabetical order (it comes in handy later) to pick up a grammar and a literature, bring both to my desk, sign his own name, and write each book number.

While the student was doing that, I was writing his two book numbers on the little white class card I had had each student fill out the first day. If this method sounds cumbersome, that's because it is, but it saved lots of arguments and many dollars at the end of the year.

Two things should be impressed on students when their books are issued. One is that they should write their names, the current school year, and their teacher's name in the front of each book. (Often, textbooks are used so long that the provided spaces are all gone. In that case, students must write the information wherever they can on the inside front cover.) It's a good idea to point out that writing the information can save them the price of the book.

Another thing they should understand is that you will not be able to accept from any student any book except the one whose number he and you have both written. Kids who realize the effect on their own wallets will give you much better cooperation in this matter.

A little trick that can also save one's pocketbook is to record in some secure place (such as the back of the card where students have recorded their books) the serial numbers of any books you *don't* issue. Then if your stock of "spares" disappears, at least you know why your count is short at the end of the year, and for what particular book(s) you are looking. Of course, when a new kid arrives later in the year, you have to remember to delete his book numbers from your list of spares.

At the close of one school year a student brought me a book with the whole stamped inside front cover gone. It looked as if someone had taken a wet towel and rubbed it off. Of course the book number was gone, along with all the names and dates.

The kid was greatly affronted when I told him I wouldn't be able to accept that as the textbook I had issued to him. He insisted that the damage had been done the night before. He was studying during dinner, the innocent lamb said, and dumped his spaghetti inside the book. He was only trying to clean it, he said, and had accidentally rubbed off the front records.

Why should I argue with a kid over a damaged textbook? Administrators make a lot more money than I did, and enforcing the rules is one of their functions. I wrote him a permit to see the assistant principal in charge of textbooks. I told the kid I was sure some fine must be charged to cover the damage, and he must ask the assistant principal to decide how much. The boy came back a little later with a receipt showing that he'd paid for the book.

If a student turned in a book numbered differently from the number he and I had written down, I checked all my book cards (it really doesn't take long to run the eye down number columns on five big cards) to make sure it wasn't my book, issued to some other person. If it was mine, of course, I kept it anyway, without crediting the kid. If it wasn't mine, and kid said he didn't know whose it was, I kept it and passed it along to the other teachers who had been using those texts.

Too many times, I'm sure, the school winds up with the "lost" book turned in as an extra by some teacher and with the money paid for that book as well. Why should that ever be allowed to happen when teachers who are short of books have to pay for each lost one—even when the books are going out of adoption?

Some books I never ordered, just to avoid the liability of having to pay for them if they got lost. Dictionaries, for example. Those things cost a fortune each. Almost every time a teacher orders a class set of dictionaries, she winds up paying for some of them that have disappeared. Why? Four or five dictionaries, bought for 25 cents each at a garage sale, were plenty for my classroom.

Other books I never ordered were teacher's editions. If I needed a teacher's edition of the grammar book, I'd be ashamed. If I wanted help with teaching the literature, the publisher was glad to mail out free resource books. I kept one for each grade level at home; they belonged to me. If I ordered a resource book to use at school, it stayed locked in my desk all the time I wasn't using it.

Workbooks are a pain to issue, a pain to keep up with, and a pain to account for. Nevertheless, you'll probably wind up using them most of your teaching years because you have to if all the other teachers on your grade level are using them for your subject. If you have to use them, the best answer is to have the kids pay for them.

A recent statute prohibits teachers in our district from insisting that kids buy workbooks, but a majority of students can probably be talked into paying for them. You need to keep ironclad records as to who has paid and who has not, so that at the year's end you can demand the workbook back (in decent shape, too) or the money. Our workbooks don't have serial numbers because they are considered "consumable"—whatever that means, exactly.

Money collected needs to be recorded most carefully and delivered to the office most speedily. The bookkeeper has lists for you to fill out and will give you a receipt for the cash as you turn in it.

2

DOLING OUT
DISCIPLINE

CLASSROOM CONTROL

A classroom is not a democracy. Sometimes I reminded my kids that they were there because of what they didn't know, and I was there because of what I did know, and that is not an "equal" situation. I might and did ask their opinions or even their advice, but my decisions were final, and they didn't have to like it.

In general, I tried to enforce school rules. Even if I ignored some violations, students shouldn't expect to get away with rule breaking forever. Putting our subject matter first and rule enforcement second, I still got around to implementing most of the rules most of the time. By the time kids came to me, they'd been in classrooms long enough to know that no teacher is either perfect in discipline or perfectly impartial. They respect a teacher who tries to adjust an unfairness when it is evident.

Chewing Gum

I was stricter than most. No teacher can possibly catch every gum chewer and punish him or her equitably. The kids knew this as well as I did. Yet I couldn't tolerate the ill-bred, open-mouthed popping and smacking that most chewers indulge in. I was brought up to believe that decent people chew with their mouths closed and make as little noise about it as possible. That's the way I explained my position on gum to the students. I would stop the ones who were the most offensive with their chewing, and chronic offenders would get conduct cuts "at my discretion." In other words, chew at your own risk. Most seniors accepted this attitude cheerfully enough. Often an entering student would walk up to my wastebasket, dump his gum, and grin, "See? I remembered. You're the one who doesn't like gum."

Asked to explain why chewing gum is against the rules, most school authorities I know mention that careless disposal of used gum messes up furniture and clothes. That is true enough, but surely a more important objection to gum is the role it plays in the spread of germs and illnesses. When I explained that to the kids and they didn't understand, I asked them to run their hands along the wooden undersides of their desktops. They wouldn't do it. They knew what gooey wads were stuck there.

No Pals Needed

Every so often we got a substitute who decided to be a real pal with the kids. Recently my kids told me about a sub who said, "Call me Bob," and became cross with one girl who kept forgetting and calling him "Mr. Brown." He wouldn't have been flattered if he could have heard the students' summary comment on him: "He was a weirdo." Kids don't need the teacher to be a pal. They have a classroom full of pals. They need the teacher to be an authority figure.

One day I came home from work and found my whole family—mother-in-law, husband, daughter, and our dog—grouped in the hall, staring into the bedroom where my son, just in the pulling-himself-up stage of life, stood in his playpen. Somehow the little fellow had managed to dislodge every wooden spoke on all four sides. They lay splayed out in all directions. Only the corner spokes supported the top rail. He stood there aghast, ready to howl for his lost boundaries.

Kids in school are much like that. The best, the most important thing we can possibly do for them is to assure them that they have boundaries that must not be crossed, and that we will help them keep safely inside.

How can we assume that leadership is a vital ingredient in every politician and a valuable asset in all walks of adult life, and yet not know that leadership is vital in the classroom? Where did the foolish notion come from that democratic processes are appropriate in every school situation?

Today, as never before in our history, kids need the reassurance of firm, kindly, well-informed leadership. That's why they push so hard. They have to know if their teacher is too pliable. The ones they respect are the ones who stand firm any time the boundary line of acceptable conduct is pushed.

Don't Yell

"Yelling at" is the students' term for any kind of correction, even a whispered one. As a matter of fact, I didn't yell. Within dignified limits, I might raise my voice to overcome momentary babble and restore quiet. The rest of the time, I found that *lowering* the voice for a reprimand is a lot more effective than raising it. It gets the kids' attention better and holds it longer. They had to be quiet to hear me.

It is just basic good manners to listen when someone is talking to you. That is the premise on which I ran my classroom. It doesn't work merely to quiet the noisier kids; they must all be attentive. Just stopping and looking at the talkers works most of the time. Chronic offenders I moved, either to another place or—a drastic measure—beside my desk. There is no reason why a teacher should put up with continuous babble. Tolerating it isn't doing the class a favor. In fact, it's falling down on your job.

Losing It

Three or four times in my teaching years I had a class that combined kids in ways that were pure bad news. Just four or five kids who are close friends can trigger a continuing classroom situation whose object is teacher-baiting. If the little "gang" begins to get the upper hand so that the teacher is stung into visible anger and unwise reaction, the whole class is lost as far as amiable rapport and easy learning opportunities are concerned. One can't conduct class discussions if two or three teacher-baiters are waiting to pounce. Kids who privately sympathize with the teacher can't be expected to buck the negative current. Kids in a classroom tend to go to the lowest common denominator where conduct is concerned.

Sometimes transferring one or two ringleaders to other classes will work. Sometimes just moving them around in the room will ease things. Sending conduct notices home is effective, but risky. One parent took umbrage at my asking her to remind her daughter that "manners are learned at home."

A device that worked well for me when I could persuade the parent to do it was to have the parent come "babysit" the student for a whole class period. As I explained, "Very likely your child will be a perfect angel while you are there. I hope so. That will give me a day's rest. But if he behaves the way he usually does, you'll see what I'm complaining about and you won't have to take my word for it."

It's surprising how far-reaching the effects of a parent's visit can be. Usually that child behaves better for a long time, maybe permanently. There is also a noticeable sobering effect on many of the other kids.

Why shouldn't parents be expected to come to school to correct their kids' behavior? If they didn't get the job done at home years ago, I was doing them a favor by letting them have another crack at it on my time. I couldn't get on with my job of teaching English until they had done their job of teaching manners and morals.

Sleepers

In any discipline situation, a teacher must bear in mind that her main obligation is to the majority of students in the class. Administrators get upset if they find a student sleeping in a classroom. I tried not to let anyone put his head down, but if it became a matter of interrupting 30 people 10 times to keep 1 kid awake, I didn't think that 1 kid was worth it. Instead, if the sleeping was chronic, I sent home a written notice or called the parent.

Sometimes a kid explained that he worked after school or for some other reason ran short of sleep on a regular basis. If the teacher doesn't believe the parent will take steps to correct a situation like that, a trip to the counselor is in order. Most counselors try hard to know and help their students. They know how to persuade parents.

Misbehaving

Some kids consistently and purposefully misbehave. This kind of student does not usually attract a true classroom following, though even the best kids are easily tempted to laugh at successful bad behavior. Still, the kid is an isolated problem. He may use every kind of unacceptable tactic from impertinent answering back after reprimands to blowing spitballs through a pen shaft. One cure for this type is to move him—up to the teacher's desk if she can stand his proximity or to the back of the room if she can't. Usually, the other kids are grateful to have their backs to such a character. If he continues to misbehave, they can pretend they don't hear him.

Every experienced teacher knows bad conduct of every kind is far more than just a nuisance that must be handled. It is symptomatic of some kind of distress, deprivation, or desperate need. I also knew that my obligation was to 150 kids per day. When I spent an inordinate amount of class time dealing with 1 muddled youngster, I was short-changing 29 others. If there is 1 bad apple per class, that's 145 others.

It's bad enough that the behavior problems were the kids I thought about most during any school day. They were the ones who cost the most in psychic energy and repaid the least in learning accomplished. I carefully rationed the amount of class time I allowed them to occupy.

I saved sending a kid to the office with a discipline card for a last resort. I did send one for flat defiance or for totally disrupting class. Apart from those two situations, if I could manage to get the kid quiet and go on with the lesson, I kept him there and talked with the assistant principal or turned in a written discipline card on him later if the problem was that serious.

If lesser measures seemed best, I sent a conduct notice home or gave him a conduct grade cut. At the high school level, a kid who was temporarily enraged often would try to straighten out the situation when he'd had time to cool down and think. I encouraged such efforts as the best solution. Surprisingly often, the kid who comes to you to apologize and is pleasantly received and thanked will turn out to feel a special bond with you from then on.

Follow Through

No matter what direction a teacher gives, not all 30 of the kids do it. One hundred percent compliance takes repetition. For kids with really bad attitudes, it takes personal instruction, perhaps even standing over the reluctant one. It doesn't pay, usually, to ignore a kid who deliberately doesn't follow instructions. He isn't going to improve on his own. Stand over that one early and often. Perhaps he'll tire of the constant supervision and decide he might as well do it the first time.

A teacher who tires of quieting the class regularly needs to remember that nobody can learn while his mouth is going.

This doesn't mean that I required or admired a dead-silent classroom. After all, a teacher is not continuously lecturing. There are hundreds of moments when a little chat between students doesn't hurt a thing. For example, in the few minutes one takes to hand back a set of papers, kids love to find out what their friends made. Why not?

A lively discussion of a literary selection will usually start up some private conversations. These must be stopped, but gently does it. After all, literature is meant to stimulate ideas, and ideas must be communicated. If kids sometimes couldn't wait to express themselves until they were called on, I couldn't fault them for caring.

Distraction

All students love to lure teachers into wasting time. Even the most scholarly ones think this is a fair game. Teachers learn to watch out for two of their favorite ploys. One is getting the teacher to tell stories, that is, to wander off into a personal anecdote that, however amusing it may be, has little to do with the lesson. The other favorite is to get the teacher to allow a class discussion to degenerate into a long-winded debate wherein the kids wander further and further from the subject of the lesson. You have to learn to cut them off, even if the classroom is still full of waving hands.

Some kids are just plain garrulous. When two or three kids whisper privately to a teacher, "Please don't say anything, but *please* move me away from him. He talks all the time!" it is time to move, not the victim, but the talker. I had a cute little fellow named Dusty some years ago who was complained about like that. When kids kept on complaining no matter where I placed him, I finally brought Dusty up to sit by me. Then—as I should have known—he began to talk to me!

I decided the time had come for direct measures. I said, "Dusty, haven't you ever known an adult who talked so much that everyone just hated to see him coming? You know, the kind of person you might see walking along the street, and you'd duck into the nearest store to get away from him? Somebody who just goes on and on until nobody can stand him?"

Dusty considered. "Well, yes. My mother," he said.

Some afflictions can't be cured.

DISCIPLINE PROBLEMS

Old hands try hard to cope with discipline problems in the classroom. Of course, when a kid really wants a trip to the office, he'll keep on until you have to send him. He'll deliberately disrupt class or create a situation wherein he openly defies the teacher. That's the time to write out a discipline card and wave him out the door.

What is disappointing is having to receive the kid back into class the next day with a note from the assistant principal saying, "Give him a P in conduct." If a P in conduct were going to solve this kid's problem, I would have given him one in the first place and not sent him to the office.

I've heard assistant principals in faculty meetings asking teachers please not to send kids to the office for trivial reasons such as "came to class without materials" or "gum chewing, fourth offense." I agree. Those little matters certainly should be handled by the teacher, but the agreement should work both ways. I won't send the kid to the office for trivial offenses if they won't bounce him back to me unrepentant because he received a trivial reprimand when I did send him.

"Make sure you're not part of the problem," someone wise wrote about school discipline. Counselors sometimes know why a kid starts giving trouble. I also tried to check in the lounge to see if the mischief maker was getting crosswise with his other teachers. Ninety-nine times out of 100, if I was having chronic trouble with a kid, so were his other teachers.

There aren't a lot of things an assistant principal can do as disciplinary measures these days. Teachers need to bear that in mind. He can authorize a U in conduct, that being the worst possible mark. Too often, the kid who is a discipline problem doesn't care what conduct grade he receives. He isn't a member of school clubs anyway because he doesn't meet the other requirements, such as good grade averages. If he's a chronic problem, his parents also have become accustomed to Ps and Us on his card, so that isn't much of a threat.

One doesn't hear much about spankings in schools these days. They do still happen, but most schools won't use corporal punishment without first offering the parent the chance to forbid in writing this type of discipline. If there's a "no spanking" letter on file, the worst kid in school can't be whipped.

I was rather glad to see the use of spankings diminish. I never thought they did much good, and it seems to me there is something wrong with hitting any person over the age of puberty in order to change his conduct. After all, it was his mind, not his body, that originated the offensive behavior.

If Us and corporal punishment don't work, what is left? There is suspension for 1, 2, or 3 days. Indefinite suspension does happen, but rarely. The trouble with any suspension is that many problem kids regard it as a mini-vacation. This is especially true when the student is allowed to make up work he's missing. That has been happening often lately with suspensions. It doesn't make sense to me.

Surely the best chance to change a kid's bad conduct permanently is to make it costly for him in terms of his grades. Also, why should his teachers be punished by the extra work of giving him makeups?

Today's students often admire these "macho" types who display obnoxious behavior. Punishment by school authorities is more likely to make a kid a hero than to disgrace him in the eyes of his peers. We need to make his conduct cost him where it hurts. If a teacher is required to do this kind of makeup, I think it's fair to be as rigid as the rules permit. The teacher should set a time that has maximum convenience for her and demand that the kid show up or take a zero.

There is an "incorrigible kid" rule on the books somewhere. I've never had to invoke it, but I think it says that a teacher who documents a certain number of episodes of unacceptable behavior for one kid is then entitled to eject him from her class permanently.

Before a teacher uses this method of pest control, she should make sure her school's administration approves of such action, that it isn't going to lower her evaluation later, and that it won't reflect on her classroom control. Better to tolerate the student than to lose evaluation points.

The best preventive for discipline problems is planning lessons that involve everyone. Don't give the kids time to think up bad stunts. Keeping them busy and paying close attention to them during every class will usually keep problems from cropping up.

Detention is worth what it costs a teacher in extra duty time. In most schools detention duty is rotated so that it isn't a big burden on anyone. This is a miracle cure for most chronic tardies. I kept thinking I'd try its effect on students' other bad habits, such as not bringing books, paper, or pens to class, but I never quite hardened my heart to make the experiment.

When it's your turn to keep detention, remember that the more strict detention monitors are, the less likely kids are to want to repeat the experience. Sending teachers are supposed to give them detention assignments to keep them quiet and working. If they claim they have nothing to do, have something on hand they can copy or an exercise they can work on. If it's fun for them, they'll be back.

AS BAD AS IT GETZ

Twice in my teaching career I have had a class of slow learners. That was two times too many. Each time the class was ninth-grade level. Both times there were fewer than 20 students in the class, as opposed to the 28 to 35 one might have in regular class. Each time, that one class exhausted me daily more than the other four (regular) classes did, combined.

Slow or *basic* or *CVAE* or *correlated*, whatever such classes are currently labeled, they are the stepchildren of the public schools. Materials for them range from scanty to nonexistent. Some educators contend fiercely that these slow learners must use the same books the regular classes do, with the teacher intervening to choose study units they can handle by repacing the material, by summarizing, by interpretation.

Lots of well-meaning social planners seem think we're meeting the needs of "basic" children if we just keep them in school. I've never understood that point of view. These kids, it seems to me, are the ones who should be tested out of liberal arts schools at the seventh-grade level, if not sooner, and placed where they, too, can experience success: in vocational institutions where they can concentrate on learning skills that will support them, without their having to carry the guilt and shame of knowing they are expected to attain unreachable heights of proficiency in English, math, or science.

I say "unreachable heights," though, of course, the truth is that more students are in basic classes because of their bad behavior than because of the lack of intellect. Still, does identifying the cause of their academic inadequacy matter so much when the bare fact of their repeated failures has already placed success in college or in the world of ideas out of their reach?

Many of these kids have been for years the foci of heartbreaking efforts on the parts of parents, counselors, even psychiatrists. If the experts can't move them to shape up and learn, I can't expect to succeed with them at the middle or high school level.

If you are assigned a basic class, as new teachers often are, don't sit down. When the basic students enter the room, put away your purse and any other articles of value. If you are using the board, have the material already written on it when the kids come in. That way, you don't have to turn your back on them. Walk up and down the aisles most of the time. *Never* get as far away as across the room from your grade book. Better still, never have your grade book on your desk.

I forgot that rule just once. The worst kid I've ever tried to teach— I'll call him Moe Getz—was in a desk close by mine because there was no other place in the room where he could be for 5 minutes without making a disturbance. Moe frequently fell into boiling rages at other kids in the class, sometimes for reasons I could not figure out. He was muscular, a football player, and when he threatened any of the kids with violence, I took it seriously.

I should have noticed that he didn't bother anyone for the 6 or 8 minutes that I remained away from my desk.

My grade book caught my eye the minute I returned to it. Moe had taken my red pen and marked over the test grades by his name, changing 45, 52, and 37 to grades in the 80s and 90s. He hadn't had time to work on the blue ink writing grades or the penciled daily ones.

I was furious, but I knew that betraying that kind of emotion to those kids would be catastrophic. I went on with the lesson until I felt calmer. While the kids were busy writing something, I leaned over to Moe with the grade book. "Moe, just look what some idiot has done to your grades," I whispered. "Every one of them has been marked over. Of course, you know that means an automatic zero for each one. Did you ever hear of such a stupid thing?"

Moe looked rather sick. I didn't give him a chance to reflect. "In fact, the only way I can prevent you from having a zero for each grade is to write them all over again from your own test papers," I went on. "Where are they?"

It took considerable shuffling and most of the rest of the period, but he handed them over. I recopied the 45, 52, and 37, handed back the papers, and marked out the changed grades. That was the last time my grade book appeared on the desk during that class.

Another time, Moe incited a girlfriend to appear at my shack door and say that she was Moe's sister and he was needed at home immediately. I chased her away by demanding to see her office permit, but I failed to get her correct name and couldn't pursue the matter to find out what class she was skipping.

On a day when Moe had pushed his tardies to the breaking point and knew that detention hovered over him, he showed up 20 minutes late to class with a permit. It was the only permit I can remember Moe's ever having. Supposedly from the art teacher, a maiden lady, it was signed "Mrs. Jones." The crowning touch was the message on it.

"Moe Getz was kepted out of your class to hep me."

I'd like to think I was as memorable an experience in Moe's life as he was in mine, but I doubt it.

DRUGS

When I was a kid, two or three boys in our senior class got drunk during our class picnic and hayride. The rest of us were horrified. What would their folks do? What would the school officials say? Would they be expelled? To our surprise, they survived and graduated. Still, their wicked exploit left an indelible mark on all our minds.

In just a couple of generations, how did we move from that kind of innocence to a society wherein drugs are in every school in the district, including the elementaries; where reformed dopers are congratulated and feted as if they were some kinds of public benefactors instead of self-centered egoists who have finally (perhaps temporarily) quit driving their relatives crazy; where our country has declared a war we seem to be losing on our desperate, dangerous drug problem? What happened?

I don't know the answer, although I was teaching through most of the years when the drug problem was building up. It still mystifies me how any human being above cretin level can ingest an unidentified pill—or a handful of pills—and expect to survive the consequences. Adolescent rebellion is a normal feature of any society, but this is fantastic.

Some teachers claim they can tell the minute a drugged kid walks into the room. I never could. Lots of kids act stoned just for fun or out of natural high (or low) spirits. Noticing that the pupils of their eyes are too contracted or expanded takes sharper eyes than mine. I'm sure lots of kids spent time in my class while they were high on marijuana or something else, without my ever knowing. That doesn't mean that I haven't seen some pitiful sights.

There was the first period class where a kid in the back of the room suddenly leaned over and spewed what looked like half a fifth of whiskey out of his stomach onto the floor. You could have gotten drunk on the smell.

There was the boy who caromed off desks on either side as he walked down the aisle to his seat. He angrily denied everything when I sent for the assistant principal, who escorted him away but told me later that he "couldn't find anything wrong" with the kid. The next day, that same boy was caught with drugs on him, and then he confessed that he'd been using them regularly.

There was the bright kid who never caused me a moment's worry. His parents, a pushy pair, invited me to dinner and told me they were worried because he only watched the other students socializing on campus without joining any group. I could only tell them he'd been just fine in my class.

They were right to worry. He overdosed later that year, was hauled out of math class down to the clinic, raving and gibbering. Another kid talked him down from that episode. Three or four years afterward, that boy came to visit me at my home. He looked terrible. He said he was living in a halfway house and felt that he couldn't stand to go home. Seeing him sit with his head hanging down, I asked if he was feeling bad. He said, "I never feel any other way."

One of the last years I taught, one of my students disappeared early in the semester. After a week or two, a counselor told me he was in a hospital for drug addiction. He re-enrolled late in the semester. He was a bright kid, attractive and full of contrition and wonderful promises. He meant to catch up, go to night school and summer school, and graduate just one year behind where he ought to have been. The hitch was, he was longer on promise than on performance. Time and again he showed up not ready for a test or with homework not done. He failed my course, but he turned up again the next fall in someone else's English class. Maybe he made it that time.

All the administrators I know about warn their teachers never to make a direct accusation to parents that their kids might be taking drugs, no matter how sure the teachers feel. Why? Mainly because of the ACLU and similar groups and the atmosphere they foster. I didn't want to be sued for trying to prevent some selfish little pothead from making dog meat out of his brain. I also knew the district couldn't and wouldn't back me in court.

What I did was to ask questions that should have made the most unconscious parent suspect something—like, "Have you noticed Jim's moods lately? Have they swung up and down more than usual? Is he more irritable, forgetful, absent-minded, excited, than usual? Does he nod off unexpectedly?"

Of course, if he was doing any of the above in class I could specify to the parent which symptoms I'd been seeing. In one case where I gave the father half an hour's worth of clues like these, the net result was that he began a campaign to have his son enrolled in special ed classes. (We used that term to identify mentally handicapped youngsters.)

Dope gets to school some way. Someone brings it. Someone buys it. Someone distributes it. None of these processes is invisible. What if we had a school-by-school campaign, using every parent who has free daytime to contribute? Those parents could be everywhere on campus that teachers, security men, and administrators aren't, every minute of the day. What if it took 1 week, 2 weeks, even months to clean out just one school? Then they could move on to the next campus. If these "parent armies" couldn't work over every school in a large district, maybe they could just keep the elementary schools clean. Wouldn't that be worth all the trouble?

Maybe judges who deal with juvenile dopers could "sentence" parents to such service. If the parents work, perhaps they could hire someone to serve in their places, or give up half their vacation time to put in their service. That would be some kind of restitution for the dangerous or deadly influence their pothead kids have had on their classmates.

We could arrange American life so that kids wouldn't have to carry money to school. There was no cafeteria in my high school. We all brought brown bag lunches from home or went home for lunch or didn't eat. Nobody starved. We didn't have drink machines or candy machines, either. The only time we needed money at school was to pay for some special thing or event: a collection for a field trip or for school pictures or some such thing. Buses can be ridden for tokens instead of silver. Lost books can be paid for by check. Dues or special fees can be handled the same way. It's entirely possible to eliminate the need for a kid to carry money to school. That could make it just a little harder on the dopers and dealers.

About all a teacher can do about dopers is to be vocal in disapproval of any kind of drug abuse. If you see any kind of behavior that is outside the norm, it shouldn't be ignored. At the least, make a note of it. At the most, send the kid to the clinic or to the assistant principal with a discipline card worded to make it clear to the receiver that you think the kid is on drugs. Code words to that effect can be agreed upon in advance, say, at the next faculty meeting. I would never put it in writing that I think a doper is a doper. No pothead is worth losing your job for.

If I don't sound sympathetic enough or horrified enough about student drug takers, that's only because I've gotten used to the idea. I was appalled. I would have done anything useful that I could think of to prevent kids from encountering such things. I hope the day will come when we look back on these years of drug abuse as some kind of mass madness that once swept over us and then went away again. Until then, all we can do is let our students know that we care.

As I began to write this section, I realized that all my experience with drug abuse in my classroom has been with boys. Twice I've learned after the event that some girl in my class had used drugs. I've heard of girls who overdosed, but never saw it happen. Neither have I ever had a classroom encounter with a girl whom I knew to be high on anything. What does this mean? I have no statistics to offer. Your guess is as good as mine.

"CHILDREN ARE DECEITFUL"

Years ago I went to a neighbor's house to explain that her three bad kids were teasing my little girl, mainly by lying to her and tricking her. I expected the neighbor to be embarrassed and horrified and to promise to investigate immediately. Instead, she smiled at me tolerantly and said mildly, "You know, children are deceitful." The mother's role became a lot easier for me when I accepted that painful truth. Knowing that fact has made teaching easier, too.

Homework

A very large percentage of homework is copied from one kid or another. Often a teacher could (if she had the time, which she never does) trace maybe 30 homework papers back to, say, six or eight original workers. That is one big argument against assigning homework at all. An even bigger argument for continuing to assign homework is that your job may depend on it.

If your lesson plans don't show homework assigned, you can be in hot water with your school administration, your school district, the state education agency, even the state legislature. All those people truly seemed to believe that my little darlings went home each evening, pulled out their notebooks, and faithfully did my assignments. It didn't take the pizza stains on some of their papers to make me realize that lots of homework gets swapped around at lunch tables, during homeroom, or in other classes.

I didn't grade homework very often. I did grade it sometimes, especially when it called for subjective responses that couldn't be copied without being obvious. For example, the assignment might be to read a poem and write a short paragraph explaining its main idea. Kids who are dumb enough to copy an assignment like that are also dumb enough to copy it word for word. When that happened, I didn't waste time and energy trying to find out who was the cheater and who was the cheatee. I wrote some message like "incredible similarity to another paper in your class" on *both* papers and split the grade I would have given it between the two, or put a very low grade on each.

Technically, I was entitled to give zeroes for any type of cheating, but if it meant I'd have to spend time investigating and trying for two confessions (or arguing with irate parents), I came out ahead settling for the process above. School administrators are notoriously weak in supporting teachers in that sort of situation, but I've never had a kid argue about the lowered or halved grade.

Writing Assignments

If kids cheat on your writing assignments, it's your fault. There's no way a kid can copy (or get someone else to write) a paper that must be done in the classroom. Even if the kid who goes home with a writing assignment doesn't actually get someone else to write his paper, what about the father or mother or sibling who reads it and points out his mistakes so that he can recopy it? How is the kid going to learn from his mistakes by having me mark them and by correcting them in his composition folder, if his mistakes are all wiped out at home before I ever see them? Want to make any bets about how much learning he gets out of home correction?

I remember vividly going home with a girlfriend in our high school days and dictating to her, complete with punctuation, a book report she handed in the next day. She was delighted and so was I; I was absolutely enchanted with my own composing ability. It was years before I realized how I was short-circuiting my friend's chances to learn by her mistakes. I hope she never thought about it like that.

A teacher of seniors explained to me not many years ago that she had each student sign a statement to the effect that he had done all the composition himself on the final exam essays she allowed her classes to take home. She was chagrined later when it came to light that one kid was selling essays to her other seniors. He charged $8 a paper. She was dismayed—but she still continued to send essays home to be written!

Some kids are adept at cheating on tests and seat work. The ones I *didn't* worry about were the kids who loved to relate fantastic tales about cheating methods: tapping out answers in Morse code, wig-wagging signals with hair, and the like. Those are the innocents who take it out in talk. The real sneaks are quiet about it and very, very clever. I braced myself for a certain percentage of cheating that I wouldn't be able to prevent, but I did what I could.

A good idea is to have two or more tests, even if the information on them is the same. This will cut down on the cheating from one class to another. You can also hand out different tests to different rows (or to individuals) in the same class. Just make sure you have some foolproof way of remembering who took which test when you're ready to grade them! Always try to have a completely different test for the makeup students. Rarely will you have every student present on test day.

Little Red Numbers

A useful device is to have your mimeographed test sheets numbered. Then you ask each student to put the number of the test paper he is using in the upper right corner of his notebook paper. That cuts down on having test sheets walk out the door. You should be seen putting the mimeographed sheets back into number order as they are handed in, at least most times. Then the kids believe you're checking all the time.

I used to have students exchange papers and do some of the grading, especially with daily grades. I didn't let them grade anything in my last years unless I had some desperate need to get a grade faster than I could do it at home. There are so many different ways of cheating when the kids do the grading. You never know whether there really was cheating or whether a certain student might just have been sloppy or stupid at grading. There are kids, too, who are sharp enough and fast enough to make a perfect or near-perfect paper while the grading is going on, and then hand in the redone paper instead of the original one. I've had it happen.

Walking up and down the aisles during testing helps. So does having students move their chairs farther apart before they begin. Usually some student will ask, "Don't you trust us?" when you begin to separate them. I learned to say cheerfully, "Of course not! What did you expect?" They always accepted that philosophically. Can't blame them for trying a little psychological intimidation right at first.

It seems important to me that a teacher should learn and accept the "children are deceitful" dictum without letting it sour her relationship with the youngsters in her charge. Think of it this way: There's no such thing as an honest baby. Honor is a concept that has to be learned over a long period of time. A kid has to make sure of survival before he starts to worry about the fine points of character.

Some of my kids each year were already the very souls of honor. Others lied, cheated, and maybe even stole routinely. The majority of them were honorable most of the time. It's easier to teach the ones who are already honorable, but you have an equal obligation to the others.

3

PONDERING
PAPERWORK

YOUR GRADE BOOK

Every grade book I've seen has a little square for each day of the week and as many weeks' spaces as make up the grading period, whether that is 6 or 9 weeks. I've never kept grades in chronological order. Starting at the left, I grouped daily grades in pencil, leaving every other vertical column blank so the grades would be easier to read.

Test grades in red ink I put in the middle of the grade book. Miscellaneous grades, which for me meant compositions, reports, oral work, and that sort of thing, went on the right in blue ink. Also for ease of eyesight, I listed students' names in small batches—three or five—and spaced between them as much as the class enrollment allowed.

It is very important to be able to go back and identify any particular grade, so at the top of the page, over each column of grades, I wrote a word or two to make me remember what that grade was for. The date of the grade I didn't worry about. If a student, trying belatedly to make a grade sheet (he was asked to make one at the start of the school year), wants to know the date of any particular grade, there are always kids around who can tell him.

There are easier and perhaps better grading systems than the one I used, but I was used to mine and it seemed as fair as I knew how to be, so I didn't change. For what's it's worth, this is the way I did it.

No Majors and Minors

I didn't have "major" and "minor" grades. I averaged the daily grades, arrived at a number; averaged the test grades, arrived at a number; averaged the miscellaneous, arrived at a number. Then I just added the three numbers, divided by three, and that was the kid's grade.

Test grades remained more important than dailies though I never doubled them, because I made sure I had more dailies than tests. The same thinking applied to their miscellaneous grades. I considered student writings our "product," and therefore worth as much as test grades. There were fewer compositions than daily grades, too.

Doing grades my way meant making four averages to find each kid's grade. Thank God for calculators! Averaging used to be easier before our state legislators decreed that every grade had to be a number, not a letter. That affected all my miscellaneous grades. I don't think I could do grades now without my little pocket calculator.

Security

You need to know where your grade book is every minute of every day. Toward the end of the grading period, when its loss would be disastrous, you should carry it with you everywhere. Never should it be left on the desk, even momentarily. I never left it locked in my room overnight when it had more than two or three grades in it. That's a risk nobody needs to take.

What should you do if the grade book does get lost? Everything you can think of. I'd begin by telling the administration. It isn't going to make them happy with you, but it's that important. You may need an administrative decision as to what to do about giving grades for that 6 weeks. If they leave it up to you, here are some steps you can take.

- Retest over recently covered material.
- Take up grade sheets from each student.

- Take as many more grades as you can possibly get in the time remaining, even if you have to let students exchange papers and do some of the grading themselves. This may net a good many inaccurate scores, but not as many as you have with no grades at all.
- Make an appeal in each class for the return of the grade book. Sometimes this works.

Turning It In

Some schools have teachers turn in their grade books at the end of each school year. Some don't. If your grade book must be turned in, it should be sufficiently legible so that a counselor or an administrator could consult it and get answers for a concerned parent. Make sure that what you marked on the grade sheet agrees with the numbers in that book!

My Way

Some people kept their absences and tardies in their grade books. I've never understood how they could do that. I had enough trouble seeing the grades in those little bitty squares, let alone extra marks. I kept my attendance records on big textbook distribution cards, as I've described elsewhere. My grade book was for grades.

Their Way

During my last few years of teaching, word came from On High that all teachers *must* record absences and tardies in the grade book. It was an even bigger debacle than I'd thought it would be. Luckily (and typically of a school district) the year after that the administration (Downtown) had their noses rubbed in how much trouble they had caused, and the tardy records rule was modified.

Recording absences in the grade books was still required the last time I looked. What it means is that you have to use two or three horizontal lines per kid to get all that information down (excused, unexcused, etc.), and good luck on retaining your vision!

GRADING PAPERS

Look at a school parking lot any afternoon when faculty members are going home. For every empty-handed teacher, you'll see two carrying papers. Considering only English teachers, make that five to one. When we don't have sets of tests, there are seat-work exercises, pop quizzes, homework, or compositions to grade.

It's terrible psychology to keep carrying ungraded sets of papers back and forth. For every day of distance between the time the work is handed in and the time you grade it, that stack grows and gets harder to tackle. Any old hand will tell you to get at it. If your family takes up most of your home time, put in at least half an hour a night on grading.

If you can, get to school 30 minutes or more ahead of the bell and grade a little each morning. I used to know a teacher who graded during each 5-minute passing break, all through her off period, and during lunch. It was probably hard on her digestion, but she carried home fewer papers than the rest of us.

Scantron Scantily

A Scantron machine is a lovely thing that grades your whole stack of papers in a New York minute. Kids color in choices from A through E on special Scantron sheets. The teacher puts a key through the machine so it will know the right answers and then pops through her test papers as fast as she can shove them. Used on both sides, a Scantron sheet has 100 answers. Other designs have lines on one side so that part of the test can be short answers or single words that the teacher will grade by hand.

In spite of the instant grading, I used Scantron tests only a couple of times a year because I knew that multiple choice or true-false quizzing usually didn't involve a student in the more complicated mental processes we'd like him to use.

Memorize the Key

When part of your quiz takes true-false or A-B-C answers, you can quickly memorize the key. Look at it this way: If you have 10 yes-no questions, you have to memorize only the spots where the 4 yesses go. Any other yes answer is wrong. Even if you give different tests to different classes, the inner parts of the tests can be identical. That way, you can zip through five sets of papers, grading only, say, 10 answers per paper. Back you go, another segment memorized, and zip through again. You'll have all five sets graded faster than you'd believe.

When students do answer true-false questions, by all means insist that they write only the initials, T or F. It's a hundred times faster to grade single letters than whole words. You'll have to make sure the kids know you'll mark as wrong any letter that can be interpreted as either a T or an F. They all know that little trick and will try it on you unless you warn them off first.

Compositions

Grading compositions was the hardest part of my job. There can be quite a discrepancy between a student's mechanical skills (spelling, grammar, syntax) and his ability to conceive ideas. I always put two grades on a composition: one for thought content and the other for mechanics. The mechanics one is easy. Follow your red marks.

The thought content grade is the difficult one. How much originality do I have a right to expect from a high school youngster? Was the subject too difficult or too easy? Did I lead them too much or too little in class discussion? Does this kid's home life handicap him in writing about this particular topic?

I suppose it's inevitable that one grades a set of themes under constant influence of the papers one has already read. Perhaps this isn't all bad. If all the papers were unusually poor, it might have been my fault, and I should ease up on the content grades for that set.

Making a composition assignment specific enough without literally writing the paper for the students can be tricky. It's easy to spot it after you've been too vague. When lots of kids keep asking for clarification of this or that point and you feel yourself getting frustrated as you try to make them understand, you probably need to rethink the objective(s) you had in mind.

Try not to mind when a student catches a grading error you've made. If it's a paper you graded by memorizing a key, you need to ask if anybody else's paper is affected. Even if there are half a dozen or more, keep smiling. You've made a mess and it's up to you to clean it up. Isn't that what you would expect of a kid?

ATTENDANCE RECORDS

Keeping track of absences and tardies is as annoying and time consuming as it is important. Every teacher I know hates the job and feels put-upon about it. I have heard that some schools in our district have efficient methods that take just a minimum of the teachers' time and effort, but I've never seen a very good method close up.

Texas bases its contribution to a school's finances upon the attendance—actual bodies present—recorded for one particular period of each school day. For as long as I taught, in our district that was second period. At that period only, a blue (sometimes white, green, or whatever) slip was sent to the attendance office. Different schools vary as to what must be written on that slip. In addition to the students' names, sometimes their grade level is required, sometimes their ID numbers, sometimes homeroom section numbers or homeroom teachers' names.

Whatever the requirement is in your school, learn it early, get it right, and do whatever it takes to get that slip in on time daily. Given the fact that when you are evaluated, you're supposed to begin a dynamic class session immediately after the tardy bell, catch and hold the class's interest, and continue a powerhouse lesson for 55 minutes, it is easy to see that stopping to record absences (and to look up ID numbers and homeroom teachers) can be hazardous to your assessment.

The best thing to do is to pray that you don't get evaluated during the second period. If you are, my advice is to get the lesson started and find a way after 15 minutes or so to divert the kids' attention (to a textbook or to something on the board, maybe) long enough to riffle through the cards and be seen noting attendance. If the whole process takes too long, jot down what you can on the blue slip and get it right after the assessor has gone his way. This is where keeping an up-to-date seating chart proves its worth.

In our system, three unexcused tardies equaled one unexcused absence during some years. Later, this was changed. After that, we were not supposed to know the difference between excused and unexcused absences. Teachers are supposed to record all absences on the grade sheets. It's supposed to be the rule in our district that the sixth absence during one semester calls for automatic failure of the course—unless there is a student-parent-administrator conference and the student is excused.

Theoretically, every subsequent absence of that student called for another such conference. In practice, the student in most of our district's schools can continue being absent as many times as he pleases, so long as each absence is accompanied by a written excuse from a parent or a guardian.

In some schools, if you follow the rules and send warning letters home after the fourth and fifth absences, you are expected to fail the student for the semester, and the administration will back you up. In other schools, you don't get backing. Check with old faculty hands before you get out on that limb. Keep a careful record of absences, but hold off on the warning letters if the building administrators aren't going to follow through for you.

Time and again I sent letters demanding that the student and parents come for a conference and then received an "all clear" notice from an administrator. Sometimes kids pile up 10, 15, 20, or more absences per semester and get clearance for everything. Then they get to tie up your early morning or afternoon time for makeups. The only person penalized for those absences is the teacher.

Where is the best place to record attendance? Not in the grade book, as far as I am concerned. I had enough trouble finding room for my grades and keeping the book legible. Some schools have teachers use attendance cards for each period. If they don't, and you aren't forced to use your grade book, try keeping your attendance on a big Textbook Distribution card.

You have to write each student's name on the card, of course, but once that is done for each class, there are miles of space for putting the absences and tardies. I noted, too, the date of any letter or unsatisfactory notice I sent home about attendance. When I noticed a student was missing, I wrote the date beside his name. That's an absence. If he came in late, I circled that date. That converted it to a tardy.

A big advantage of the master card method of attendance recording is that one can see a whole class's attendance habits at a glance. It isn't necessary to look at 30 individual cards to see who needs a letter or a notice.

EXCUSES

Probably a lot of forged excuses have gotten by me. I'm no handwriting expert and wouldn't, in most cases, know the particular parent's handwriting well enough to recognize it. I did look with suspicion on an excuse signed "Mr. Jones" or "Mrs. Smith." Most adults are too well-bred to sign themselves like that.

Having looked with suspicion, what did I do about it? Depends. Sometimes nothing. For example, in our district a kid can be absent five times; whether excused or unexcused makes no difference. The sixth absence, however, *if unexcused*, is supposed to mean automatic failure. Also, each three unexcused tardies add up to one unexcused absence. (That was true some years; some years it was ignored.)

Classroom teachers are supposed to record all those absences and tardies on the back of the student's attendance card and to mark them on grade sheets to be printed on the report card. I did all that. However, the few times I tried to pursue the matter of that sixth unexcused absence by sending the student to the office to make his or her losing course credit official, the student came back on each occasion with "continue for credit" noted on his permit. Some parent had shouldered the blame again and convinced our administrators to let the kid get by with breaking the rules.

Usually it is the homeroom teacher's job to keep excuses. After each classroom teacher has signed the excuse, the kid returns it to the homeroom teacher. Most of us toss excuses into the hole behind the right lower double desk drawer and hope we never have to fish for them again. I have seen it happen, though.

What do you do when a kid hands you a parent-written excuse that says "car trouble" or "family business" or "we went out of town"? None of these, according to our district policy, are supposed to be excused absences. In theory, we excuse a student only for a death in the immediate family or his personal illness. In practice, you have neither the time nor the administrative backing to insist on identifying all other absences as unexcused.

Why fight it? I just wrote the parent's exact words, in quotation marks, on the back of the attendance card. I let any student make up work if he cared enough to come in early and do it. If I thought his absence was unjustified, I could give him a harder makeup than the original test. This wasn't usually necessary, however. His missing class probably meant he missed enough instruction to make it harder for him, anyway.

Recent district practice is to suspend a student for 2 or 3 days for misconduct—and then to allow him to make up any missed grades! This infuriates teachers, and rightly. Why should they have to give extra hours making up troublemaking brats who ought at least to have to suffer the consequences of their misbehavior?

Parents who truly irritate me are the ones who decide that it isn't any of the school's business why their kids missed school. Between the district's hard-nosed stated policy and the paranoid parent, guess who is caught in the middle one more time?

Like so many little teaching tasks, keeping records on attendance too often turns out to be all responsibility and zero clout to enforce the rules—on students, on parents, on administrators. Seasoned teachers roll with the punches on this one.

LESSON PLANS

When I started teaching, nobody in junior or senior high wrote lesson plans. We used to smile sympathetically when elementary teachers moaned and groaned over their eternal plan-making. Not for us! The old hands had their routines in their bones. No need for anything on paper. As a newcomer, I used to make a little list to keep myself organized. For a grammar lesson, it might read, "1. ck. homewk. 2. notes on bd. 3. Prac. 15, p. 263. 4. Warn quiz." Then the Texas Education Agency, or God, or someone lowered the boom.

For years, every teacher in our district had to use the same lesson plan form. For each day of the week, there was a 15-inch horizontal swath divided into blocks. A tiny block to the left must have the ELO number, that is, the number of the Essential Learner Outcome the teacher hopes to achieve by means of that day's lessons.

In the large block next to the ELO number, the teacher had to spell out what the ELO is. Entries in this column had to begin "Students will . . ." and then state the ELO. For example, ". . . trace plot in a short story." To save myself the irritation of writing "Students will" five times per week, I just wrote it very large in the Monday block and let that serve for each following weekday. Department chairmen saw to it that all teachers had copies of their subject matter ELOs. Couldn't keep school without 'em in those days.

The next block on the lesson plan form was the one that counted. Here the teacher wrote the activities she wanted the class to do that day. It's always better to plan too much rather than too little. Just remember to go back and put check marks to show which activities really got done. I wrote a P for "Postponed" for anything I didn't get to. Then if it was still worth doing, I put it in again as soon as possible. Plans had to be turned in weekly or biweekly. I always made a carbon copy to keep on hand.

That wasn't the end of the lesson plan. The next block required the teacher to list the resources she needed for that lesson. If there were mimeographed papers, notes on the board, student papers being used, they had to be listed. Nearly always, one would list the textbook(s) that she had issued.

After that block, the next called for a number (from a legend at the bottom of the form) that indicated which teaching techniques were to be used for that lesson. A 10 was for evaluation, 9 was review, 8 was lecture, 5 was supervised study, and so on. The only hazard that I saw about that block was that one shouldn't indicate the lecture method too often. Lectures are out of fashion. I usually listed two or three numbers. For instance, we might have a brief quiz (10) and then a short lecture (8) followed by a discussion (4).

Farthest to the right was the homework column. For me, it was the hardest one to adjust to when I had to start making and turning in plans. Planning a week or two in advance to arrive at a certain spot in the textbook so that a certain homework exercise can be assigned on a certain day is a chancy business. Most of the after-the-event marking and changing I did to my lesson plans was in this column.

How seriously should a conscientious teacher take lesson plans? Just as seriously as the administration in your school makes you take them. If you notice, as I did somewhere along the line, that the well-established old hands didn't turn in plans, do likewise as soon as you feel you have the status to get away with it. Of course, you have to plan lessons. No one can teach without doing just that, but these lockstep, show-and-tell written plans are among the more grievous affronts that intelligent teachers suffer. Luckily, during my last years our district seemed to have forgotten about them.

Written plans that are of value should be made and kept in the upper right-hand drawer at all times, and you should probably have at least two alternative plans for each kind of class you have in case you are absent. These plans should call for activities that won't interfere with the lesson sequence you are conducting at that time.

For English teachers, a simple in-class composition (paragraph or so) works well. Some kinds of grammar review exercises are good. If you're out for 2 days, the sub can have students exchange the composition papers and mark each other's grammar, spelling, and punctuation errors. Rewrites are then in order. Substitutes truly appreciate finding plans that really work and can be narrowed or expanded at need.

UNSATISFACTORY NOTICES

We had a districtwide policy that one did not put an F on a grade sheet unless the student's parent or guardian had been notified. It's a serious mistake to break that rule.

It happens often, maybe every grading period, that some student will slip below the passing level without the teacher's being aware of it. With me, it happened if I checked a borderline kid's average at notice time, which is about halfway through the grading period, and decided that he or she was going to pull it up. A percentage of those kids you count on to pull up just don't. Also, kids who have been absent don't make up the missing grades as you expect they will. When your student load is 150 kids a day, you miss a few things like that.

When the time comes to put down the grades, you want to give that student the F he deserves. My advice is, don't. If you haven't sent the parents a warning, go ahead and give the kid the lowest possible passing grade. Next grading period, you'll be alert to that one. If he gets by you twice in a row, it's your fault.

We had the kind of notices that make their own carbon copies—two, in fact. Kids sign and date the notices, then pull off the top copy to take home, get signed, and return to the teacher. Both carbons are kept by the teacher, one to give to the counselor and one to keep on file. There are two or three lines of demographic data to be filled out on the top part of our notices. Most of us let the kids fill out those lines before the copies were separated.

It's important to follow through on the carbon copies. Chances are, you'll never see the top copy again even though it is meant to be taken home, signed by the parent, and brought back. The fact that it never gets back to you won't matter if you're protected by the signed copy you kept plus the one you gave to the counselor.

Lots of kids get notices every grading period, never take them home, and get by with it because they do manage to pass. They're the ones who need that extra motivation of a threatened F to get them moving. You'll see a marked improvement in their performances once the notices are handed out.

Don't forget to read the notice if the parents do send back a signed copy. Sometimes parents write notes to the teacher on those copies. Usually such a note will ask for a phone call or a conference. You can keep these second, time-consuming contacts to a minimum by putting lots of information on the unsatisfactory notice. I put all the grades the student had earned up to the notice date. It's also wise to put absences and tardies if there are enough of them to be affecting the kid's grade. Unacceptable conduct should be noted, too, in dignified but concrete terms.

Parents can't be blamed for not understanding notations like "He is obnoxious most of the time" or "disrupting class." They don't explain enough. Better say, "He picks on other students until they ask to be moved" or "talks back when reprimanded" or "often interrupts with irrelevant comments. Tries to entertain class." For most parents, your complaint won't be the first they've had on the kid. Most of them will be honest enough to tell you so.

Remember, unsatisfactory conduct notices can and should be handed out at any time in the grading period when you need to let the parents know. I find them more effective than a telephone call, especially since often the call doesn't put you in contact with the person you want to reach. Just bear in mind that you must choose your words carefully. Somebody loves this monster and is ready to believe his classroom problems are all *your* fault.

There's no good day to hand out notices. Just before Christmas is the worst time, but they're just as necessary for that grading period as for any other, and waiting till after the holidays usually won't allow enough time. I tried to hand out all the notices for a class on the same day. Even then, there were usually some I had to hold over. The kind of kid who gets a notice is the same kind of kid who is chronically absent. Then there's the worry of remembering to give the absentees their notices when they do return.

When I made out an unsatisfactory notice, I put a pencil F by the kid's name in a column of my grade book. When the kid signed the notice and took the top copy, I circled the F. Then I knew, without having to dig for the notice, that it was safe to enter a failing grade on the sheet for that kid if he did fail. During final exams, I made it a point to check the actual signed notice if the kid was failing the whole semester.

It's hard for adults to realize just how disorganized and illogical kids' minds can be. Their reactions to unsatisfactory notices illustrate this graphically. I have seen kids who hadn't made one passing grade the whole semester turn livid with rage or display absolute astonishment when I handed them notices. I suppose some of them really do expect miracles to happen for them at report card time.

One way that a failing grade can sneak up on a kid is this: Perhaps he failed the first grading period, making, say, a 60. Then he passed the second time with a 72. Suppose he makes a 70 the third time. Good so far. That failing grade is so far behind him at this point that he may have forgotten it entirely.

You are not obliged to send him a failing notice for the last (third) grading period if you see that he is going to pass that time, but in my district there were five grades to be averaged in order for the kid to pass or fail a course. The exam grade and the proficiency grade are still to come, each of them equaling 20% of the whole course grade. Where proficiency exams are not given separately, of course, there would be only four grades to average.

If that kid makes a 65, say, on your final, he has to make an 83 or better on the proficiency. He has to make 350 points, any way he can, in order to pass the course. Yet because he didn't fail the last grading period, he didn't receive an unsatisfactory notice. I tried to be alert to the cases where this situation was likely to arise and to warn the endangered kids that it was possible to fail a course without last-minute notice.

Some teachers have a policy of handing out notices to each student they teach. Then they never have to worry about whether parents were notified when they have to enter an F. I just never have had the time to prepare that many notices, except for one grading period years ago when our principal insisted that we send notices to everyone. I did it somehow, but I felt put-upon for 2 weeks afterward. The parents of successful students didn't like it, either.

ALL KINDS OF NOTES

This section deals with both kinds of notes: the right kind and the wrong kind. I put the right kind on the board for students to copy. I take up the wrong kind every time I see them being handed around.

The Right Kind

To college professors, the idea of putting notes on the board to be copied probably sounds ludicrous. Their concept is that students know how to sift lectures into meaningful jottings as they listen. Maybe college students do know how to take notes on their own. If they do, I'll claim credit for having taught them by example.

Grammar units in textbooks are set up in long, drawn-out chapters. They always start with the easiest material and work up to areas of greater difficulty. Nothing wrong with that, except that by the time students reach sophomore level or above, they are turned off on grammar anyway, and the first easy pages of a chapter on, say, verb tense, convince them that they know all about this and won't need to listen. They are ready for a boiled-down, compact set of notes such as I put on the board.

With verbs, since there is so much to say and to know about them, I made a chart of the four principal parts and then drew a conjugation chart on a different part of the board, putting labels across the top for six tenses and down the left side for the six persons and inserting the permanent tense helpers in the appropriate boxes.

When students looked at a conjugation chart on the board, it was easy to impress on them that the third person singular present tense form of the verb adds an *s*. I put an *s* in the appropriate box and explained that since we have no logical excuse for adding that *s*, they must simply memorize that we do it that way.

Kids will swallow down large chunks of idiosyncratic practice with the subject matter if one explains honestly that this or that practice is "just the way it is." Warning to beginning teachers: "Just the way it is" won't work as a substitute for "I don't know." That's cheating. The dullest kid in the room soon will realize that the teacher who uses that trick can't be trusted.

I insisted that students keep their notes all year. They come in handy not only for review before finals but also in teaching other parts of the subject matter. For example, they needed to take another look at the four principal parts of verbs when we studied verbals. I could point to the fourth column of their charts and show them that all gerunds come from that column; all participles come from the third or fourth columns; all infinitives from the first column, preceded by "to."

Different kinds of notes fit different units of study. My notes on clauses waxed discursive. In sentence form I grouped all the generalizations that can be made about the different kinds of clauses. For background notes on the short story, I might list and define words and phrases: *rising action, theme,* and so forth. When we did the *Odyssey,* I put names on the board and expected students to add sufficient definition to each while I taught the background information to them so that they wound up with adequate memory aids.

In this Xerox age, a new teacher's first impulse may be "I'll just photocopy all that and give the students handouts." Of course, handouts are quicker and easier. I used them, too, but only when I was going to read and discuss with the kids every item on the handout, and when I believed the kids would appreciate the importance of the material. Believe me, in a lifetime of teaching you will never be able to convince 100% of any class to read any handout you give, not even if you make one offering free tickets to a rock concert.

Notes I had students copy from the board were the ones I thought they would otherwise shrug off; the ones they wouldn't be paying attention to during discussion. I figure that when their eyes have to see the information and their hands have to copy it, to some degree at least it must make an impression on their brains.

The Wrong Kind

Students who wouldn't do a writing assignment on a $100 bet sometimes are your most copious writers—of notes to other students. I have often regretted that all the communicative energy kids put into their personal notes can't be channeled into legitimate composition assignments. Of course, if we somehow legitimized private note writing, the magic would be gone.

This is not to say that I allowed private note writing in my classes. No lesson plan I ever wrote included time for private notes, and I resented the impudence of a student who ignored instructions and spent his class time on his personal correspondence. I took up all notes I saw, including the ones that were in transit across the room.

Next question: what to do with them. I *never* read a note at the time I took it up. Sometimes other kids urged, "Read it!" This could mean they are just avid for possible scandal. It could also mean they know the note contains a "fooler" for the teacher—a bait note, intended to be taken up and read so the class could have a laugh at my expense when I would read, "Ha ha, Teach! Fooled ya!" or something similar. I put any note I collected inside my desk or inside my purse. When I forgot and just tossed a note onto my desk, often it disappeared when that class filed out at the bell.

I read each note for two reasons. One is that it might contain references to drug buying or using that ought to be relayed to the assistant principals. The other reason is that it might contain a suicide threat.

The first time I took up a note that threatened suicide, I kept it 2 or 3 days, thinking over the situation, before I discussed it with the school nurse. She was an amiable woman whom I had never seen angry until then. She was really upset that I had waited so long to tell her about it. "We *never* take suicide threats lightly," she said. This was years before the recent rash of school shootings. That lady was ahead of her time.

In that incident, she talked with the student and found that the bad home situation had eased, so that nothing more needed to be done. I'd learned my lesson. After that, I always relayed a suicide mention to the nurse the same day I learned of it, even if it was inconvenient for both of us.

What is in the vast majority of private notes? I used to brace myself, expecting to read a tirade about how horrible I was, perhaps some lurid and explicit references to my personal and sexual habits such as one finds on desktops from time to time. Nothing so interesting has ever shown up.

In fact, 99% of students' notes ignore the existence of teachers. They are solely concerned with their personal relationships. Girls write to girls about their friendships, the falsity of other friends, betrayals, and revenges. Girls write to boys about sex. Favorite themes are "You are just using me," and "Can't we be together again?"

Boy-written notes are less common, but they do happen. Boys usually write to boys about specific plans: "Let's cruise Saturday night," or "Can you go with us Friday?" Once I picked up a long love note that a shy boy had written to a popular girl. It was most touching. I longed to tell him he had a flair for poetic expression, but, of course, he was already humiliated that I had taken up his note. The kindest thing was to let him hope I had destroyed it unread.

I did destroy all the notes that weren't specifically dangerous enough to pass along to authorities. It seemed to me that my taking up the notes was sufficient punishment, so I did nothing further about them unless the writer offended again and again.

One day I picked up a note from a girl who was a chronic discipline problem in small ways. I had already had to call her down two or three times during that period. She had just written, "This teacher is about to make me slap her." I hadn't even been conscious of my danger.

TESTING

In recent years it has seemed as if the state and our district were competing to see which could push more new tests onto the kids faster. Recently, each of our high school students was double-tested at the end of each semester. That is, he took a 2-hour proficiency test in each academic subject and then a 2-hour final given by his own teacher.

TEAMS, TABS, TAPS, MATS, TAAS, TAKS, and Iowa tests are some but not all of the other standardized tests high school kids take. Of course, there are also PSAT and SAT tests for the college-bound, as well as APs. If necessary, SATs can be taken again in the hope of making higher scores. To the above tests, add IB finals, oral and written, on subsidiary and higher levels for honors students. They will probably also take the advanced placement tests, hoping to skip some of the basic college course prerequisites.

The teacher must add to the tests listed here frequent testing over units of subject matter. Each teacher is free to plan as many or as few tests as she thinks necessary. I liked to figure in three or four tests for a third of the 6 weeks' grades, along with 8 or 10 daily grades and 3 or 4 on composition.

A dangerous aspect of testing is that the easiest tests to grade probably are the poorest measures of students' learning. One can whiz through stacks of true-false, multiple choice, or matching, quickly memorizing the key. It's often tempting to test literature with such handy methods. I added at least a section of short answers or an essay question or two if I was going to count that paper as a test instead of just a daily quiz. Just for finding out whether students have read the material, the easy graders are sufficient, but identifying character traits or motivations and drawing inferences or evaluating ideas from the whole selection require more sophisticated methods.

It isn't smart to use the same test all day if you have several classes on the same grade level. If the third period consistently does better on the same test than first period does, but you can't detect an overall superiority in intelligence, someone is probably passing along the answers—or at least the questions. I always handed out numbered test sheets. If the number sequence was incomplete when I handed them out, the students never knew that. I asked students to write the test number under the date on their papers. I made sure they noticed me putting returned test papers back into number order.

About those mimeographed tests: I have small patience with teachers who hand out tests and let kids write on them. It's an extremely wasteful and completely unnecessary practice. Why shouldn't kids write answers on their own notebook paper? The only advantage I can see for teachers' using disposable tests is that in grading them, the teacher can line up the answers physically. That probably makes grading go a bit faster. However, grading T-F or A-B-C answers goes so fast anyway that one doesn't really need the answers to be aligned perfectly. Once the teacher uses up that set of tests, she has to spend the time she saved running it off again. I've weathered too many paper shortages to believe the little gain in grading speed justifies the waste of paper.

Good testing, like good meal preparation, requires careful planning. A teacher ought to ask herself, "What do I want this test to prove?" Simple recall is not a complicated mental process, nor is it one we need to stimulate continuously. Much more important is training students to ask why, to categorize, to evaluate, and to extrapolate. In short, they need practice in making judgment calls. Is this more true today than formerly because we're so self-conscious about "judging" nowadays or even noticing differences? Maybe.

One thing I'm sure about is that people are not born with values systems. They develop them slowly, and the adolescent years are crucially important ones in that process. Teachers need to be in there, helping the values systems form. Testing can be a vital factor in this development.

Because our kids are being tested so much these days, and also because the end of the grading period often fails to coincide with the end of a study unit, I don't favor giving a "6 weeks' test" per se. What is the logic of giving a test because a certain number of school days have passed? No teacher I've talked with likes the idea of giving a 6 weeks' test. Counselors do.

Counselors take courses about tests and measurements. They run their schools' standardized testing. Pretty soon they get so immersed in, and so expert about, *how* to test that they may stop asking themselves *why* to test. Most of the teachers who have discussed the matter with me just don't give a 6 weeks' test if the counselors don't insist. If the counselors do insist, the teachers often give one of their regularly planned tests and label it "6 weeks' test" on their lesson plans.

A teacher's own tests should always be graded promptly, and not just to impress or please students, who start asking for results about an hour after they've taken the test. If the philosophy of giving a test is that the teacher and the student need to find out what he does and does not know about the material recently covered, then surely both of them need to know where he stands as soon as possible after that material is finished. For the same reason, a test that was worth giving should be a test that is worth going over in class.

Since there are always absentees on a test day, usually more than on nontest days, a teacher has to figure out how to go over a test that Jim or John or Jane didn't take, with Jim or John or Jane now sitting in the room, listening. Even if (as I hope she will) the teacher plans to give a different version of the test to the absentees, still the material will be about the same in most cases.

The teacher can make one of several choices: postpone going over the test until everyone has taken it (I did that sometimes); she can give such a radically different makeup test that it doesn't matter (I did that sometimes); or she can send those absentees to the neighboring teacher's room for the time it takes to go over the test (I did that sometimes).

TARDIES

Students will be as tardy as you let them be. No matter where on campus your room is located, it will be difficult to reach at some period for some kid. Apparent "hardship" cases usually can be cleared up by a brief conversation with the chronically tardy kid or his parent. Sometimes the student just needs to change his route or the time he goes to his locker. If he really has to, he can get to your class on time.

Don't look to administrators to control tardies for you. They really can't, especially in senior high, where Eros beckons around every corner and walking somebody wonderful to his or her locker rates a much higher priority than making class before the bell. What you have to do is to make tardiness unattractive to the kids.

I kept a composition book on my desk and just motioned to a kid to sign it anytime he came in tardy without a permit. I made no exceptions. Neither written nor verbal explanations were allowed. The kid just signed and sat down, thereby interrupting class as little as possible. I entered those tardies on the back of their attendance cards daily, if possible. Let a week of them pile up, and it's the devil's own job to make all those entries.

It doesn't work to keep the tardy book anywhere except on your desk. If it's across the room, the kids will fake signing, sign phony names, or make deliberately illegible signatures. The bolder ones are likely to add a remark or two about one's personal habits!

Does all this sound too rigid for senior high? Just try teaching without controlling tardies. You'll find yourself losing from 5 to 15 minutes of each class period in interruptions as students stroll in, explain, and expect you to backtrack over whatever ground you've already covered. Even the most conscientious students will forget punctuality when they see you don't prize it enough to enforce it.

I know of one other thing that works. Two or three times a year, administrators get excited about the fact that the halls are clogged with students after the class bell has rung. They decide to enforce tardy procedures. Occasionally, teachers are allowed to (or even encouraged to) lock their doors when the tardy bell rings. Students stranded in the halls are then herded into a central location and given whatever disciplinary action the administrators see fit to hand out.

Such a "sweep" works beautifully. For a week or two, the halls will be clear. One sees students actually sprinting to class. The trouble with it, of course, is that administrators soon learn that keeping the halls cleared is a full-time job. Pretty soon they drift back into their normal occupations, and the halls are dotted again with ambling, gossiping, flirting students.

A side issue that surprised me about the tardy book was the discovery that kids don't see anything wrong with signing each other's names. Two kids would come in together, tardy. One would say to the other, "Sign my name, too." They were amazed when I reacted indignantly and gave them a sermon about the unique nature of one's signature. It seemed to be the first they'd heard of it.

Class should be started right after the tardy bell has rung. If the first thing on the agenda is a spelling test and you dictate a few words before a late student strolls in, so much the better. Just seat him where he can't get the missing words from nearby pals. His lower spelling grade is a punishment that fits the crime. He probably won't be late on your spelling test day again.

A by-product of strict enforcement is that soon your students start getting to your class on time, even if they're habitually tardy the rest of the day. You'll hear, from time to time, remarks like, "Tardy? So what? She never notices." Just be sure that doesn't describe you! In a few weeks your tardy book entries will be down to the few chronics.

There are things you can do about these incorrigibles. Most schools have policies that allow a teacher to send a student to detention after three or four tardies. You can try sending home an unsatisfactory notice just for the tardies. You can cut conduct. In most schools, a P (for poor) can be given without office permission. For the lowest mark, U as in unsatisfactory, an administrator must approve. It's usually easy to get approval on documented chronic tardiness, and sometimes it's worth the trouble.

I don't recommend calling parents on absences or tardies. Experience has shown me that irresponsible children most often have irresponsible parents. In fairness, let me add that legally, home and school divide responsibility for our children during each school day, and it's pretty hard on parents to try to control class attendance when they can't be there to track each kid. We teachers are in a lot better position to enforce punctuality than parents or administrators are.

MAKING COPIES

Using a modern copier is the most expensive method of duplicating materials. Good old duplicator masters and those awful machines that get your fingers purple and require fluid and love to jam wads of paper are the more economical method. Most schools I know about have had to assign only one or a few persons to run some of their photocopy machines. They also require a record of which teacher requested how many photocopies of what.

If copiers are assigned for general teacher use, teachers can be given code numbers so that the machine will cut off when they have used their semester quotas. These are necessary measures. Teachers really abused the privilege when those nice, clean, dry, clear copies first became available. I have seen teachers copy whole books.

Except for final exams and very special materials that would take forever to type, I used the old duplicator masters and machines. Recently I learned a good trick from a colleague: Put the duplicator master into your typewriter upside down. Then when you make a mistake, you can roll up that line, reach inside between the bottom ends of paper with your razor blade, and make the correction without having to remove it from the typewriter and then try to get it back into the right spot for typing over.

Why should teachers make a separate copy of a test or a quiz for each student to use and later throw away? I made a class set and used it over and over—it saved an endless amount of redoing time. Also, I made at least two versions of the quiz or test. It cuts way down on the cheating when kids feel pretty sure you're using different versions at different periods. It's also a good idea to label the sets A and B. Then they know for sure. Of course, if you're desperate and have time to make only one version, by all means label it B or even C. Then they don't know for sure.

In our district, English test day is Monday. That's why Monday was the worst day of the week for me to go to the workroom to run off a test. Often there was a line of other last-minute teachers ahead of me. It's much better to plan ahead and use the machine during one's off period some other day.

About old yellowed tests and exercises that you've cherished for ages: Kids do resent the idea that they're dealing with "old stuff." If the information is still valid and the test questions are still pertinent, consider doing a little retyping at your convenience now and then. You can get by with a few such antiques per semester, but if all your materials look out of date, so will you.

PROFICIENCIES

Time and again, our district huffs and puffs and announces a new, killer test that must be passed by every student. This test is meant to ensure that every graduate of our school district is highly skilled, fluent, and literate. Then when the test is actually produced, we discover that somebody has chickened out. The test is at such a rock-bottom level that any student at higher than moron level could pass it. English proficiency tests are like that.

When the tests first came out a few years ago, we trembled in our boots, hoping we had taught enough subjects well enough to get by. We soon found that not only were the English tests ridiculously easy but also the grading was curved to an incredible degree. One had to be trying with both hands to fail, to avoid making a passing mark.

They have lessened the curving quite a bit, but the semester-end proficiency test is still easy. The only students whom I can justify for failing it are the foreign students who still have too big a language barrier. I'm told the proficiencies in math and science are more difficult. It's only the English proficiencies I know about.

A considerable hazard is the fact that many errors crop up in the English proficiencies. One year I made a written protest through proper channels because one of the questions had no correct answer. Students were asked to choose among four sentences the one that was grammatically correct. None of them was. The one intended to be chosen began with a coordinating conjunction. My students complained to me about this question.

After a couple of weeks, I received a reply from one of the test makers. The gist of his response was that while it was true that "many English teachers" still consider it an error to begin a sentence with a coordinating conjunction, "everybody does it that way." And ain't that the truth!

4

THINKING OF TECHNIQUES

GET THE HOOK

No matter how much we may regret it, teachers today are, as never before, expected to be entertaining as well as enlightening. It's all very well to say, as I often did, that I was not getting paid to sing and dance for the kids. The fact was, I needed to do whatever I could to make my subject matter interesting and exciting for young people who had spent many hours of their lives turning on what interested and appealed to them and turning off what didn't.

A teacher ought to take stock periodically to see if she's acquired any off-putting mannerisms. As much as any other group of people, teachers are creatures of habit, and these little things can creep up on one without being noticed. Two bad habits that I battled from time to time were playing with a rubber band as I talked and rolling up pieces of paper—permits included. I thought I was keeping my little tricks suppressed pretty well, but kids soon learned never to leave a permit on my desk. Wise ones stood right there until I signed and returned it.

There's no excuse for looking sloppy, either. Gone are the days when a teacher could get by with a dangling slip or tornado-struck hair just because she was an authority figure. These students are used to seeing people on television who are not only well-groomed but unusually attractive. The least we can do in competition is to keep our hair combed, our makeup straight, and our petticoats concealed.

Sometimes I wonder if anyone besides me can remember a teacher who wore the same dress straight through for a week at a time, changing the detachable collar and cuffs once or twice as she felt the need. That was when most people didn't have washing machines and before schools were air conditioned. That same teacher had one of those crinkly "bobbed" hairdos. I remember her digging at her hair with a pencil, saying she'd be glad when Friday came and she could go to the beauty parlor to get her hair *combed*. Every other week she had it washed and set.

We need to keep in mind always that what is fascinating to us may appear deadly dull to students. Just beginning a study unit with a striking statement can help. For instance, the day before I planned to teach the Herakles unit, I used to write on the board, "Herakles was stupid"—and refuse to explain it. "We'll get into that tomorrow."

That little gambit made at least some of the kids wonder why I couldn't spell Hercules and also why I made such a statement about their Superman-like television cartoon hero. When we got into the unit and they became acquainted with the real character and career of the old Greek, they learned three things: television versions of the classics are not to be trusted, not all heroes are like grown-up Hardy boys, and not all good stories have happy endings.

There are "hooks" to use to get students' attention for grammar units, too. Beginning a discussion of participles, I asked students to close their eyes and picture a cat sleeping—eating—clawing—running. Reminding them that "to modify" means "to change"—as when they "modify" a car—I got them to discover that the words that modified (changed) their picture of the cats were all verbs. How can verbs be modifying? What parts of speech are supposed to modify?—and on from there.

As you go through the year and practice inventing "hooks" to create interest in the lessons, you get faster and better at it. If it doesn't take much to turn off kids from a lesson, it also doesn't take much to turn them on. It's your business as a teacher to keep looking for the magic words. They're there somewhere.

HOMEWORK

Is it really necessary, not to mention wise, to assign homework every night of the week? I've worked for principals who would accept nothing less. I know counselors who insist that every student should have 30 minutes' homework in each of four academic subject areas every night. What does that mean for the slow worker? How about the kid who has an after-school job?

I do believe in frequent homework assignments. (It's a lot easier for me to believe in them now that my own kids are grown up.) I just don't think they have to be long, and I liked to skip a night every now and then. The argument I used on reluctant parents is that homework is the students' practice just as much in English as it would be if they were learning to play the trumpet.

Nobody expects the music teacher to grade all that practice, but it must be done if the student is to learn to play that instrument. This should be explained to the kids as well as the parents, because the more conscientious ones tend to feel betrayed if they do the work and it doesn't get graded. In fact, even the lazy ones who only do one assignment out of five feel betrayed if you ignore the assignment they did do.

Homework that I *had* to assign was some of the reading. In the higher level classes, most of the reading had to be done at home. Otherwise, we'd never have gotten through all the literature in the text, let alone anything extra. It's hard for me to feel that asking a person to read is asking him to *work*, but one must keep in mind that reading still is work for many of the students. Their constant cry is, "I don't have *time* to read!"

I told the kids that's why they make the side of a bathtub flat on top—so you can put your book there and read while you bathe. Read while you eat. Read between things. Read while you wait for something or someone. Read at the orthodontist's. Read on the bus or in the car. I read while I cook and while I do the dishes. Girls can read while they roll up their hair. Put a book on your lap when you're going to watch television so you can read during the commercials. If you get lured away from a sitcom or a game show into a good book, you'll be ahead.

Sometimes I graded homework. I tried to wait for the kind that can't very well be copied. These were daily grades, and I tried to get enough of them so that any one daily grade was not very important. It seems to me the most important aspect of homework is not just the bit of subject matter that can be gleaned from any one assignment, but the development of a continuing expectation of work that must be done at regular times at home as part of a student's living routine.

WRITING ISN'T HOMEWORK

Writing of any kind should never be sent home to be done. The minute that assignment goes out the door, you've lost control of who does the thinking, the organizing, the grammar, the spelling, and the punctuation. Every one of these skills is necessary to the student, but he's almost sure to get outside help in the areas where he's weakest, if he doesn't simply beg, borrow, or steal someone else's writing entirely.

Beyond all those factors, you've lost control of the student's use of time when a paper goes home to be done. Students, especially the most conscientious, think they're doing the teacher a favor if they spend 4 or 5 hours on a writing assignment that ought not to take more than two class periods, if that long.

Somebody has to teach kids that work, including writing, has to be done within time limits. Adults who take Tuesday, Wednesday, and Thursday to finish Tuesday's work, are likely to be fired on Friday. I'm not talking about rushing through, or rewarding hasty, careless composition. Nobody knows better than I that flash cards are inventions of the devil. I give no prizes for excessive speed. I just know that at least half the kids I teach will dawdle endlessly over a two-page essay if they aren't pushed.

One of the sayings for which I was infamous among students is, "The way to get through on time is to start." Requiring a rough draft, as I always did, along with the "good" copy helps here. A kid is more willing to begin a rough draft because (to his way of thinking) it isn't such a commitment as a good copy is.

Why should only English teachers require writing to be done in class? Any teacher who asks for a summary, a report, or anything at all to be written in sentences faces the same problems as an English teacher does about assigning written work to go home. I believe that if all teachers always required writing to be done in class, we would have far more accurate ideas of students' composition skills and needs than we have now.

Some teachers may be horrified at the idea of giving a whole day, or 2 or 3 whole days, "just" to student composition. Why? Any one of those teachers probably would gladly spend a period, or two or three, on showing films. I *never* showed films in English class. How about *Romeo and Juliet?* For English students, it is to read, not to look at. That goes for the rest of the wonderful and not-so-wonderful movies of great books. Students can and will go to see them on their own. It is far more appropriate to use class time for learning to compose readable essays.

While students write, you can sit and watch, ready to answer individual questions as needed, or you can walk up and down the aisles. Lots of students will have a question or two for you if you are near their desks, whereas they might not bother to get up to ask them. Give them the opportunity. It's only fair to help that much.

LEARNING PREVENTION

Sometimes I asked my kids, "Why do we go to such lengths to avoid using our brains?" They all knew what I meant. Every human does, but nobody seems to have the answer. The phenomenon is at its worst in the classroom. Perhaps it will help to specify a few situations that militate against the desired result of brain work.

Rigidity

Students enter a classroom ready to assume an adversary position at the drop of the teacher's hat. Beginning teachers often are told, "Don't smile the first 6 weeks." Truly, a beginner has to guard against being too easy, but at least equally important is the establishment of an atmosphere in which a student can feel free to ask questions and to discuss what he has read.

Such tactics as insisting that a hand be raised before a word may be spoken, or that students never speak to each other between activities, seem counterproductive to me. I think a dead silent student is either asleep or wishing to be.

Not Earth-Shaking

Not everything I wanted to teach my seniors was critically important. For instance, I didn't lose sleep nights if they didn't seem to get much of a "take" on the Anglo-Saxon poetry in our anthology. I didn't fancy it much myself. Just to know it's there was all I asked of them. If they didn't understand the plot and characters and the gorgeous poetry of *Macbeth*, however, I suffered from the grumps until that situation improved.

One thing every teacher ought to do for her kids is to put the subject matter in perspective. It won't breed contempt in a student of American Lit, for example, if the teacher reminds students that in the early days of our country, a little over 200 years ago, even the greatest minds had little time to devote to literary pursuits. If the harvest in the anthology looks a bit scanty, that is why.

Above all, we should not be hypocrites about the parts of our curriculum we don't admire. If you think a particular selection was just barely good enough to make the anthology, or a unit of math or science is of doubtful value, you should mention your opinion to your kids, stressing, of course, that it is *only* your opinion. It's likely to relieve their minds. Not everything we teach needs to be approached with reverence.

Too Much Planned

If you've overplanned a class period so that the kids don't get everything done, you have three alternatives. Let them do the remaining activities for homework, put the remainder into your next day's plans, or forget them. Letting kids see that you are willing to forget something you considered important enough to put in your plans is poor psychology. If you already have a homework assignment made, your best choice is probably to put the activity into tomorrow's work. Showing changes on your lesson plans never hurts. Proves you're using them.

Too Little Planned

Sometimes a lesson goes faster than you thought—or worse, it goes faster with one class and slower with another. Whichever happens, you can't afford to be left with as much as 5 empty minutes before the bell rings. Letting kids sit and do nothing, or babble and do nothing, for that long is demoralizing to them and painful to your nerves.

Any teacher worth her salt will look at her watch and say something like, "Oh dear, we have only 5 minutes left, and I was hoping to get in a really detailed review of _____ (whatever springs to mind). Well, we'll just have to do the best we can in so little time." Then you can whip out the grammar or literature and go over some questions in an appropriate spot. If it's timely, the teacher might say instead, "Since we have only 5 minutes left, I'd like to spend it discussing _____ with you," naming a general-interest topic that concerns the whole school.

For an English teacher, alternatives to fill the gap are endless. She can say she's going to "steal a little time" for a quick survey and go into a discussion of a popular movie, a best-selling book, a local show, or a school production. She can always discuss books she has read or books the kids are reading. Sometimes these spare minutes can be so interesting that everyone is surprised when the bell rings.

A teacher soon learns that frequent injudicious planning has a bad effect on the kids. If they have too much to do often, they begin to feel harassed. Too little, and they assume your subject isn't very important. Flexible activities that can be stretched or squeezed need to be part of every day.

Put-Downs Are Pernicious

Sooner or later you're going to feel an overwhelming urge to make some kid regret an asinine opinion that he voices about something that is important to you. With me, often it was Shakespeare. God knows why, but kids who have never read two pages of the Bard feel perfectly entitled to let the class know they consider him "stupid." In fact, some kids can't rest until they say so.

Try to resist the urge to retaliate. You and I know where the "stupidity" is, but pointing that out publicly will not accomplish anything you want. It is time for the soft answer that turneth away wrath.

A kid who puts down Shakespeare is a kid who is convinced he cannot understand Shakespeare. Leading him into understanding and a modicum of appreciation is your far nobler course. The same thing is true of most other subject matters about which kids are reluctant.

Sometimes a student will sail right into a recitation and not have the least idea that he has completely missed the meaning of what he has read. For everybody's sake, you must correct his mistake. Doing it without putting him down and making him resent the intervention is the art of teaching.

It takes longer than just saying "you're wrong," but saving that kid's feelings makes an impression, not only on him but also on his classmates. This is true especially of the ones who knew the right interpretation all along. They will be most impressed that you were able to turn him around without making him lose face.

"That's not it" or "Wrong!" are words you should seldom or never use. Forget "You're missing the point," too. There are better ways to correct a student. Let him believe he was close, even if he gets no cigar.

See It Last or Never

I have never regretted that not many films are available for English classes, not nearly as many as there are for history. Films too often do great violence to the written words that preceded them. In every case I prefer to read the selection first and see the film last, if we have to see a film at all. The flavor of Dickens' *Great Expectations*, for example, is almost completely lost in the movie, though the movie itself isn't a bad production. Students who see the movie first are not likely to appreciate the book as much as those who see the movie last or never.

THE EQUALITY GAME

A tricky aspect of teaching is the situation we all face daily: If we ask a question and five hands go up, the five answers we could receive will not be of equal merit. Sean, for instance, probably doesn't even know what you asked. He is waving his hand because he wants attention first, last, and all the time, from anybody. Becky knows the answer, but she is garrulous. Every time she is called on, another 2 or 3 minutes of class time go down the drain.

Roger may or may not know the answer. If he gets it wrong, there'll be no placating him. He'll swell up like a toad and sit there hating you for the rest of the period. Susan knows the answer and would explain it neatly and concisely. Alberta probably doesn't know; she merely wants to be noticed by the boy two rows away. She won't care in the least if she's totally wrong.

What law says you have to treat these diverse persons as if they were equal? They are not equal mentally, physically, or morally. The only obligation you have is to give them equal opportunities to learn insofar as that is possible. You don't need to invite disruption by calling on students who are going to be argumentative beyond reason or resentful under correction. No rule says you have to promote the attention-getting devices of those who seek to use you and your classroom for their publicity grabbing.

Some things I did try to be scrupulously even-handed about. Reading parts in a play is an example. Usually everyone, even the worst reader in the room, wants to have a part. I usually went down rows with parts and changed to new readers each day during a play just to make the kids know I was being fair. Then if someone demonstrated total inability to handle his role or refused to take the trouble to keep tracking, I felt free to relieve him of his assignment.

PUT IT ON THE BOARD

Now that most schools have modern copiers, hundreds of clear copies of any kind of printed material are readily available to teachers. This, of course, has led to some abuses. Photocopy paper is costly compared to duplicator or mimeograph paper, so most schools have to limit how much photocopied material a teacher can request. Our school required a department chairman's signature on copy orders.

A good thing, too. Ordering 150 copies, say, of a daily quiz or a routine test so that every student can write on the photocopy paper and turn it in is stupidly wasteful. Order a class set, 35 or 40, to allow a little for attrition. Number each copy any time you use a class set of any kind. Have students write on their own notebook paper—and that one class set can last for years and years. The numbers discourage students from walking out with copies.

When I wanted the kids to have notes on any topic from Greek mythology to pronoun use and case, I put these notes on the board and asked the kids to copy them. It seems to me they must involve their brains at least a little in the process of putting the notes on their paper. In almost all cases, I talked the notes to the kids as they copied them, to supplement and reinforce the information they were taking down. I reminded them that in college they would be expected to glean notes directly from lectures without any such nursing along.

Sadly for me, the modern white boards and erasable colored pens came along too late. I never had those luxuries. Modern teachers don't know how lucky they are!

Any time I could, I illustrated a lecture on the board in some way. Visualizing the subject helped keep students' attention focused. Too, I hope it demonstrated the kind of note taking they would need to do for themselves later on.

Handing out printed material to a class of 30 regular seniors means that fewer than 15 will read it. If I stated several times that the material would be tested over the next day, maybe 18 or 20 would read it. If I put it on the board and walked around the room while I went over it with them, all 30 had to read it.

I learned during the first semester that *assignments must always be written on the board.* That is the only way you'll survive as a teacher. Otherwise you'll drown in a sea of "I didn't hear you," "That's not the way you said it," or "You didn't tell *our* class." Not only put the assignment on the board, put it in the same *place* on the board every time.

Early in the semester, announce on several different days that you don't intend to keep mentioning the assignment each time, since it's on the board. Then stop mentioning it altogether. Don't forget, though, to mention it to parents every chance you get.

Years ago I began putting a Do Today list on the board for days when we had a number of activities to cover. It proved to be such a handy device for the kids and me that soon I made such a list daily. There were separate lists when I taught different levels. The kids liked it, and I loved their not asking, one after another as they entered, "What're we doing today?"

VISUAL AIDS

Someone in the library is usually in charge of audiovisual aids. Teachers check them in and out and need to learn whatever rules a particular school has for their use.

Using the Opaque Projector

An opaque projector will show a printed or handwritten page on a screen. One can't touch the paper once it is in the projector. I used the opaque once a semester, putting corrected student papers (names concealed, of course) into the machine to show how I marked papers and to identify mistakes that are most frequently made. Warned by another teacher's experience, I was careful to let students know the papers they saw were from a different class. Otherwise, they would fret over whose paper it might be instead of focusing on the mistakes and their corrections.

This rarely happens, but the teacher mentioned above had a disagreeable session with an irate parent whose son decided the teacher had chosen his paper just to "pick on" him. I used to take the added precaution of asking students' permission to use their papers, promising not to show their papers in their own classes and to keep them anonymous.

Overhead Projectors

An overhead projector lets a teacher mark on the paper she is discussing, but she has to use plastic overlays and a grease pencil. I never found much use for this in teaching English. It was so much easier to write on the board. I think overheads were made with math teachers in mind.

Films

Films and film strips have been made to aid in teaching grammar and punctuation. How much of a learning experience are they? Given a class of 30 viewing any type of film, at least 10 of them will be napping or otherwise "goofing off" in the relative obscurity of a darkened room at any given moment. Then, too, one has to question the wisdom of giving students what are often watered-down versions of the original if you're showing films of literary selections. How much *Candide* does a student glean from a videotaping of the television musical?

GOOD ENOUGH IS GOOD ENOUGH

Perfectionists shouldn't teach. It may even be true that perfectionists *can't* teach. Every year I made sure to say during the first few days, "I believe in excellence." That certainly is true. The point kids need to see is that we are *striving* for excellence. The point teachers need to see is that something short of excellence has to be accepted in most cases.

Once, a student transferred into my ninth-grade class during late November. When I asked how much grammar her former class had covered, the girl said, "We started on recognizing nouns and we were still there. The teacher said we couldn't go on until everyone could do it." Sometimes I picture that unknown teacher, still whacking away at noun recognition with that same old class. More likely, she left teaching long ago and found some kind of work that has attainable goals.

The day when "everyone can do it" seldom comes. Most of the time we have to teach as hard as we know how for as long as we think is right, and then go on. Even if I thought that a whole week's effort had gone over the kids' heads (it didn't happen often, but sometimes testing shows surprising weakness), it usually seemed better to leave that subject for a while, go on to the next thing, and come back later, perhaps in the guise of review for a final. Often the second pass at the material will go much better than the first. Some learning really happened the first time, you will probably discover.

Perhaps you have a wonderful project idea or composition idea for the kids. You present it enthusiastically and painstakingly go into detail, and still the kids make a mess of it. It's time to remember that the concept was thrilling in *your* mind, not in theirs.

Subjective grading is always difficult. One can be fair about it only by being as *objective* as possible. Look at the effort from the student's point of view. Weigh in his different background, his shorter life experience. Is his product really as hopeless as it appeared, measured starkly against your ideal?

A teacher can't afford to set her heart on achieving a certain level of accomplishment with every kid. Somebody is always going to fall short, often for reasons that have nothing to do with you. If you are teaching well, some of your kids will perform splendidly, most of them will do respectably, and a large majority of them will pass. That will do. Perfection is for angels only. Good enough is good enough.

BARE ESSENTIALS

Too often during the year I said, "If you people don't learn another thing this year, please at least learn *this*!"—naming whatever bare essential had come to my notice just then. There are hundreds of them, things I believed my seniors should be ashamed not to know.

On any bare essentials list for high school seniors, I would include:

1. *a lot* is two words; so is *any more*
2. the plots of *Macbeth* and *Hamlet*
3. the pattern of iambic pentameter
4. that gentlemen don't wear hats indoors
5. all eight parts of speech—including their functions
6. where not to put an apostrophe
7. to use only one subjunctive verb per *if*
8. what "The Hollow Men" is
9. what happened in *The Iliad* and *The Odyssey*
10. all *four* lines of "i before e"

A complete list might grow to book length. There are so many little things kids should know and often don't. It is appalling to find out they have never heard of some of them. Worse is finding out that some of them don't care to know.

Some time ago I asked a clerk in my bank some question or other about the bank's procedures. She stared at me frostily and said, "I don't know." Not "I'll find out for you," or "You might ask that employee over there," or any other helpful thing. Just "I don't know." Then she waited for me to go away and quit bothering her. There are Bare Essentials for bank clerks, too. That girl had never learned the first ones: Banks need customers. Serving customers is what banks are for. If she ever learns them, I won't know it. I don't bank there any more.

WRITING VERSUS PRINTING

Soapbox time again. This topic seems to me a much more serious one than most people think. I believe it matters in all subject areas, not just in English classes. Our kids are losing the skill of handwriting.

In place of handwriting, they develop (somewhere in middle school, usually) much slower, much less efficient techniques of printing. Unfortunately, the kids somehow equate this "writing" with their individual personalities. Some of them print entirely in block capitals. Some use all small letters, often even at the beginnings of sentences. Most use a mishmash of block and lowercase printing. The slowness of the process makes them tend to drop letters from words inadvertently. Frequently, they throw capitalized words into the middle of sentences for no reason. It's a mess.

I am convinced that in our district the trouble begins at the primary level. In first and second grades pupils are not just encouraged but are required to print—and worse, not to print in a style they will ever use again, but rather to copy the printed letters in the books they read! Kids like my own two, who never quite mastered drawing perfectly vertical lines freehand, receive grade cuts in both "handwriting" and "reading" for their printing deficiencies. This went on with my own kids while I was receiving little thank-you notes for Christmas presents in cursive handwriting from my nephew and nieces in primary grades in Tennessee.

The argument that "small muscle development" in little hands does not allow them to write in cursive in first and second grades is so much hogwash. Think about it: Are the muscles they must use to print not the same muscles they must use to write? Neither printing nor writing by a first or second grader looks very good. Why waste 2 years making the printing look better before switching them to cursive and having to start all over again? No wonder our students never seem to get a "take" on cursive and prefer to cling to their cumbersome, slow printing as long as we let them do so.

Anyone who teaches doesn't need to be convinced that all students are much better off writing cursive than printing. When a student tells me, "I can print faster than I can write," I always believe him. What he is telling me is not, as he thinks, that he prints fast. He is telling me that his cursive is cripplingly slow from lack of practice.

Speedy, accurate note taking becomes increasingly important as the student progresses in secondary school. In college it is vital.

Faster writing is also vital in classes like mine, where all compositions are done in the classroom.

Most students' printing, being so much slower a process than thinking, leads to dropping letters from words. Then one doesn't know whether the student can't spell or is just once more a victim of his lack of cursive skill. Lots of student printing is harder to read than cursive. It is meant to be, I suspect, at least subconsciously. If you can't read it, you can't tell when it's wrong.

It was an annual bombshell when I broke the news to my seniors each fall that cursive writing was required. Some wailed, "But I've forgotten *how* to write cursive!"

I made a standing offer to help these forgetters daily before school, starting with ovals and push-pulls. I never had any takers for that offer.

How is any teacher ever going to discover the individual student's writing instruction needs when that writing goes out the door and is vetted by everyone from parents to siblings to pals before it comes back to the classroom for evaluation? With speedier and less tiring cursive writing, you can at least obtain sufficient authentic samples of your students' skills and deficiencies by having all writing done in class. That's better than never finding out what the kids don't know.

IN THE LIBRARY

School librarians love to help. Let them. They'll give you lists of audiovisual equipment and materials of all kinds. They'll pull books for your classes in advance of your coming and have them on a trolley for your convenience. They'll try to seat your group conveniently for the books they need. They'll know whether they have enough books for all your students in whatever special area you designate.

Usually, ninth and tenth graders are given a library orientation session taught by a librarian. All you have to do is to get down there with your group and keep them decorous during the instruction.

A great advantage of teaching in high school is that there are many books you will enjoy reading. I have found some watered-down biographies, and of course many of the novels are aimed at juvenile interests, but there is plenty in most secondary school libraries for an adult who is willing to spend time browsing.

If you are unlucky enough to have a floating teacher in your room during your off period, you have to scramble your papers together and get out daily at that time. The library makes a good, quiet hideaway. Usually there are back rooms where one can spread out materials and concentrate. There isn't any stale cigarette smoke, and the lighting is usually better than that of the lounge. If you also miss a few messengers who are seeking you to ask you to take some missing teacher's class—well, shucks.

In return for all these conveniences, you have some obligations when you bring a class to the library. The first is that you must stay with them. No fair giving yourself 10- or 15-minute breaks during a class period. You wouldn't take off for a break during a class period in your room. Keeping your students working and in order is not the librarian's responsibility.

Just being in a novel (no pun intended) atmosphere and out of the classroom routine stirs up the devil in some students. This is why spending a day or two in the library with each class on some long project is so exhausting. You really discover the book-haters on such a visit. If a kid simply won't look at his book after you've helped him find the right one, move him to an empty table if you can. Usually there is some place where he can be isolated and prevented from bothering others.

Romance, too, rears its giddy head in the library and must be thwarted. I separated any students who appeared to be indulging in a date on my time. They really didn't have time for a flirtation if they were doing what I had asked them to do.

Out of 150 kids, a few usually suffer real anxiety attacks when it comes to making a commitment such as checking out a book. They doubt; they hesitate; they can't decide among three or four books. They need to be reminded that this is not as solemn an occasion as, say, a betrothal, and that it won't affect the fate of the nation if they don't get the very best possible book. Their nervousness is real. They should be comforted.

It is only courtesy to ask the librarian at the beginning of your visit if she wants to say anything to your students. Any little rules she wants followed should be attended to scrupulously. In her own setting she's the expert, not you. She'll appreciate it, too, if you keep the kids reminded to return the books they checked out on time.

INDUCTIVE ISN'T GOD

Education is a faddy business. Every few years some educational entrepreneur comes around and sells the school district some wonderful new method that is going to solve everyone's problems. As a textbook salesman once remarked to me, "I could sell this district any program I wanted to—for 1 year!" That's the trouble. We seldom stick to those wonderful new methods long enough to see if they really work. When we do, sometimes we go overboard and throw out perfectly good old techniques in favor of iffy new ones. That's the way I see the inductive method.

When I began teaching in 1964, our in-service programs were loaded with lectures and demonstrations of the great new teaching device: the inductive method. Lectures were taboo. No decent teacher would be caught dead just telling the kids a piece of information. The kids must be led, step by delicate step, to discover the answer for themselves.

There is much that is attractive in the inductive method. A student will prize information more if he can feel he has found it out for himself. Also, it's a lot easier to believe a conclusion if you've worked your way to it by piecing together one fact after another. The main objection I had, and still have, to the inductive method is that it takes so long.

I never had enough time, for example, so that I could afford to let ninth graders work their way inch by inch to the discovery that we have eight parts of speech. I always just plain *told* them there are eight, and what they are. Then we had a basis for learning the fine points about them.

There are plenty of legitimate uses for the inductive method. It is particularly appropriate, I found, in our discussions of literature. Students can and should develop an understanding of character by picking out instances in literature where someone in a story is brought to life by the way his traits are shown. They should be able to make some predictions about the outcome of a story by piecing together the characters and their circumstances. They should become able to judge whether the end of a story is appropriate by considering the situations and personalities involved.

What always seemed to happen when I set out to use the inductive method was that I found I must first do some deductive groundwork. I had to define a phrase and a clause for my students before I could lead them to realize that a sentence wherein a clause and a phrase are balanced like equal parts has something wrong with it. For me, the inductive method was frequently a good Step 2. I just didn't have much luck using it as Step 1 in most units of instruction.

We've moved on to other fads nowadays. The inductive method is still with us, rather like a religion to which one still owes lip service, but which few people take very seriously any more. That's a shame. It's an excellent teaching tool, so long as it's kept in its place.

"I DON'T KNOW"

Any student, no matter how lacking in information or intellect, can quickly detect a teacher who doesn't know her subject well. Kids have an instinct for phonies. Oddly, no matter how uninterested in the subject the kid may be, he'll bitterly resent having a teacher who is not well prepared. Teachers need to do their homework, too.

No matter how knowledgeable a teacher is, from time to time students will ask questions to which she doesn't know the answer. Only one response will work in these cases. One must say, boldly and simply, "I don't know." Trying to fake it is fatal. It's best, of course, to follow through by suggesting a way that you (and the students) can find out. Sometimes it works well to ask a particular student to find out the answer and to come prepared to give it the next day.

Kids already know you don't know everything. Occasionally saying "I don't know" isn't going to damage a competent teacher in their eyes. In fact, the more perceptive youngsters will like a teacher better for her honestly admitting to the fallibility of which they are already aware.

Sometime during each school year I tried to get around to revising the kids' perceptions of the term *ignorant*. Most kids these days seem to feel that when one says someone is ignorant of anything, he's making a derogatory remark. I believe that as long as we're involved in the detection and cure of ignorance, we ought to be exact about the meaning of the word.

I pointed out that we are each born with a terminal case of ignorance, and we spend our lifetimes trying to cure as much of it as we can. When they visualize a baby in its state of near-total ignorance, kids can easily accept the term as a simple indication of a mental condition that can and should be cured.

TEACH OR TAP DANCE?

One sentence kids learned not to utter in my classroom is, "It's *boring*." Unluckily, it is the favorite word of most adolescents. As soon as the first kid said it—usually about English in general—I stopped for my annual sermon on boredom. I told them boredom is a sign of a little, tiny mind. "Morons are bored 90% of their time. That is because they usually can't track what is going on."

I drew a big circle and a little circle on the board. "Here's what my best teacher told our geometry class," I explained. "This smaller circle is the mind of a moron. Inside is everything he knows. See the rim of the circle? At all points on the rim he makes contact with all the things he doesn't know. There's not much room around this circle for contact points, so the moron is satisfied. He's sure he knows just about all there is.

"See how many contact points the large circle has? Inside is the smart person's mind. He's in contact with all this expanse of things he doesn't know. That is why a smart person is never satisfied. He's always thinking of what he hasn't learned yet."

We need to shake kids out of the rut of thinking they are entitled to entertainment 24 hours a day. Since this new pitfall was introduced by radio and television, many of today's adults have not grown up in a situation where there was no button to push that would bring instant amusement. It isn't a case of anyone's *telling* kids they should expect constant entertainment. We have *shown* them they should expect it. Many kids today, I suppose most American kids, have unrestricted access to television all their waking hours for the first 6 years of their lives. Then they go to school.

For the first time, school shows these kids they can't change channels when they tire of an activity. They have to correct, to start over, to get it right. They have to repeat over and over until everybody gets it right. When the kid is wrong, a whole class full of other kids knows he's made a mistake.

A kid in the classroom has lost his safe, nonparticipating watcher's status. He loses the prefabricated, concrete pictures that illustrate any abstract ideas he may encounter on television. In school he has to make up his own examples. Imaginations that have been stunted by years of accepting other people's illustrations now have to go to work. It's a lot easier just to quit trying and say, "This is boring!"

A teacher needs to look at the subject matter and figure out what makes it worth teaching. If the teacher doesn't know how this material will be of value to the kids in their adult lives, it's a cinch the kids won't know. On this premise, I stopped teaching transitive verbs some years ago. Never, in my own writing, have I needed to know if the verb I used was transitive active, transitive passive, or intransitive. I cannot imagine a use for that knowledge except that it comes in handy for teaching the difference between *lie* and *lay*. Hardly a sufficient excuse for including a week or two on transitive verbs in the curriculum. I gave it up sadly, even though I'd invented a really neat system for teaching transitives.

If we believe that what we teach is of value to the students, we shouldn't have to sugarcoat it. We expect too little of our children's minds. Perhaps that is why they do so poorly when their efforts are compared with academic achievements of kids in other countries.

Isn't there something sick about the way we tiptoe around our children, scared silly that we are going to bore or annoy them by asking for their best intellectual performance?

Once I took an eighth-grade class to the school library to select fiction for book reports. One girl was a recent arrival from Korea. Since she didn't command enough English to participate, I took her over to the art section and handed her a big, beautiful picture book featuring master artists. She opened it to a page containing a picture of a world-famed sculpture. Her eyes lighted with happy recognition. "Ahh! *Pieta*—Michaelangelo!" she exclaimed.

How many 13-year-old American girls know that much about the world's most famous art? And how much do you suppose that girl's Korean teachers worried about whether she was being entertained while they taught her the art lessons? Is it likely that she complained, "This is *boring*!" and if she did, would her complaint have made her teachers feel embarrassed or apologetic about their subject matter? Only in America do ignorant children assume the right to pass judgment upon subjects about which they know nothing. Only in America do adults take the uninformed judgments of children seriously.

Valid subject matter, presented by a person who believes in the value of what she is teaching, is interesting. A teacher is, in a sense, on stage in the classroom. If she expects all eyes to follow her as she presents the material, she ought to try to make herself worth watching and hearing.

At regular intervals a personal stock-taking should be in order for every teacher. Little annoying mannerisms creep up on us from time to time and need to be eliminated. One helpful private gambit is to measure oneself against another teacher's shortcomings. "He never finishes a sentence. Do I?" "She has that irritating way of giggling. Do I do that?" "Do I make eye contact without staring holes into them?" "Do I go on too long? Repeat too much?"

Especially and always, one should be on guard against televisionese. "Have I picked up any clichés lately? Do I say 'Would you believe' or 'Gimme a break' or 'I wasn't that interested' or 'We're into ceramics' or 'At that point in time'"?

Simple, standard English is preferable for all teachers all the time. Trying to keep up with the latest slang or to talk like the kids will only make a teacher ridiculous. Even if the teacher succeeded perfectly in imitating the students' style of conversation, that wouldn't make her popular or add to her credibility. Why should it? A teacher should sound like a teacher. Every kid knows that.

There are many ways to enliven a curriculum and to heighten interest in one's subject matter. I believe in using any trick that works. Why not? I just don't believe in being apologetic about or in trying to disguise the fact that my goal is to teach grammar, composition, and literature. I am proud of that.

5

MINDING THEIR MANNERS

TELEVISION INFLUENCES

Only a few decades ago, teachers were a child's earliest and most dominant educational factors outside his own parents. Now, television reaches him far earlier and occupies more of his hours than he will ever spend in our classrooms. It behooves all of us to recognize some of the thousands of things the student learns, long before any of us meet him.

There are some first-class programs for children on television nowadays. I often heard my high schoolers fondly quoting this or that item they learned from *Sesame Street*. Sometimes I thought it was the only place where they ever heard of conjunctions before. There are fine nature programs on PBS and others just as good on various aspects of science. Also in the "television benefits" column I place the news, though it is astonishing how few students, even seniors, watch any newscast regularly.

Eye Training

For a long time I've suspected that the less obvious damage television does is the greatest in the long run. For example, consider the basic eye movements involved in our students' learning to read English prose: top to bottom, left to right.

In earlier times it often used to happen that a student reading aloud would jump a line unintentionally. Nothing was wrong with the kid; his eyes just hadn't had enough practice yet in moving top to bottom, left to right. It seems to me that high school students are jumping lines now the way kids used to in elementary school. They skip words. They stumble. Their oral reading skills are way down from what students at this level used to have. Why? I think it is the same problem.

Kids who have spent hundreds of hours with their eyes flitting about erratically, watching and tracking pictures—pictured heads, bodies, hands, feet, mouths, eyes—instead of reading words left to right, top to bottom, are simply lacking in the eye training that we pretelevision people acquired in our earlier school years.

Imagination

Alarming too is the fact that they haven't acquired the habit of imagining the scenes they do read about. They are accustomed instead to seeing scenes that someone else imagined, even down to the colors, the shades of meaning, the facial expressions of the characters, the gestures. How can we possibly be surprised when our children show an appalling lack of imagination? When did they ever have the chance to exercise it?

Attention Spans

Educators don't talk as much now as they used to about attention spans. I wonder if they've just given up and accepted the idea that American children all have tiny little attention spans and mustn't be asked to do any task that takes over 30 minutes. This is another educational handicap that I blame on television. For the first 6 years of their lives, kids get used to seeing all problems solved, all situations resolved, in 30 minutes or less.

Speech Patterns

I used to be puzzled to decide which was worse: hearing kids mouth television clichés such as "Would you believe . . . ?" and "Sorry about that!" or hearing kids using the bad grammar they learned from television—for example, using *like* as a subordinate conjunction. Now I know something worse: hearing kids spout clichés that are *also* bad grammar. For instance, "I could care less," and "I'm not that interested," and "as far as . . ." followed by a subject but no verb, and "I'm into folk dancing." Another one favored by almost every television "pundit" is "different than" (as opposed to "different from").

I was happy for the lady in the ad for a medical institution who announced that her child had survived cancer with the institution's help—until I heard the lady say that "if it weren't for _____, our child *may* not be with us today." Of course she meant *might* not, but I am sad to think she is sure to instill scrambled subjunctives into that child's mind for 6 years before the schools get a chance to intervene.

Slipping Definitions

More subtle language changes are also in the fumbling, if well-groomed, hands of television personalities. They have made *controversial* a synonym for *well-known*, no matter why. *Problematic* is another word whose meaning has been scrambled beyond recognition. When a dirty movie is about to be shown, they coyly mention that it contains "adult" themes. It usually also contains "adult" language. Isn't it fun, knowing that we adults belong in a category that means nasty?

Too painful to discuss is the way CNN has totally banished all forms of the verb *to be*. No employee of theirs makes a complete statement in a newscast any more. It takes a verb for that. I suppose their executives figure that without a verb stated, nobody can claim he or she has been accused of anything. Example: "The Prime Minister today, saying . . ." That's not exactly accusing the fellow of anything, is it?

Sleazy Morality

I wish parents would take a good, hard look at the shows their kids most enjoy and make an effort to boil down to a single sentence the moral each show teaches. I think they would wind up with a list of precepts that goes something like this.

- It is all right to kill anybody you are chasing (or who is chasing you) without benefit of any formal legal procedure, so long as you are a private detective or any type of law enforcement officer or a close friend of either or a really nice person who has decided to dedicate his life to preventing evil. (The nice person gets to decide for himself what is evil.)
- It is all right to have sexual intercourse with any person at any time so long as you are a "caring" person. If others are hurt as a consequence of your sexual activities, it is all right as long as you are terribly sorry that they are hurt.
- It is all wrong, mean, narrow-minded, and ludicrously outdated to mind if someone connected with you is having sexual intercourse with other people or is living with a person of the opposite sex (sometimes the same sex) to whom he or she is not married. It is still wrong to mind, even if this is your son or daughter.
- It is all right to be pregnant but unmarried, no matter how young and insolvent you are, so long as you decide to keep the baby. Giving up the baby is not all right, no matter whether you have means to give it a home or not.
- It is all right to be an unmarried father, so long as you want to keep the baby yourself. (It is nice if you want to keep the mother also, but not essential. What makes you a nice person is that you want to keep the baby, no matter how ill-prepared you are to support it or give it a home.)
- It is all right to demand your baby back, even if it has been legally adopted and has lived with its adoptive parents for years. Of course, you must be terribly sorry for the foster parents if their feelings are hurt.
- It is essential that you care frantically about the ecology. It is not necessary to do anything about it, or to learn anything about it, but you must *care* about it.

- You should give only your first name on all occasions and call everyone of any age by his or her first name. This indicates a friendly, democratic spirit on your part. No adult deserves any particular respect, such as is shown by calling a person Mr. _____ or Mrs. _____. Use their first names no matter how young you are or how old they are or how recently you met and even if you have never met, as in some telephone encounters.
- It is a sign of sophistication to refer frequently in your conversation to urination, defecation, and copulation. In fact, one of the three, or at least the body parts connected to those activities, should be referred to in at least every other sentence.
- The point of putting a bite of food into your mouth is so that you can talk through it.
- It is fine for any child to give any smart-aleck answer to any adult, including his parents, so long as the answer is funny.

It seems to me that every teacher has certain obligations toward students who arrive in high school saturated with some or all of these items of sleazy manners and morality. It is pointless to be angry with the parents of a high school kid because they didn't teach him any higher moral concepts or social graces. He's here and we have to deal with him. What can we do?

Over a semester or a whole school term, plenty of situations arise wherein a teacher can subtly express moral ideas without making a sermon about them. There will be times when the teacher can demonstrate her own moral values. Be a role model, as we say these days.

Discussions of literature help enormously in putting across some of these concepts. In fact, most class discussions can be guided so as to include some kinds of moral precepts. I don't believe a teacher should be preaching, day in and day out. It's just that the teacher may be the only positive moral influence some kids get. We need to keep that in mind.

JUST PLAIN MANNERS

"We English teachers are forced to teach manners and morals along with our subject matter nowadays," an Ivy League professor told an English banquet audience one year, "because all the other disciplines have retreated from it." Three cheers. To put it more simply: A kid has to have enough good breeding and self-discipline to sit down and shut up before I can teach him anything.

We can probably blame television for this situation, too, but it doesn't really matter now what caused it. The plain truth is that many kids no longer feel any obligation to shut their mouths and listen when someone talks to them. I used to spend the whole year working on this.

If dead silence had been my goal, I could have achieved it a lot faster by making a total crackdown on any student who uttered a word without permission. Getting what I considered best, a modicum of peace, quiet, and attentiveness on a daily basis, took continuing effort.

At times when you are distributing papers or checking attendance or are momentarily busy with some other routine matter, don't let it worry you if a modest babble develops. If you can reestablish order by standing before the class and waiting a few seconds, you're in good shape. One soon develops a sense of how long it should take a class to become quiet. It doesn't work to allow chatter to go on too long. Students come to expect to be allowed to rattle on if you don't bring them back to attention quickly.

Grade level makes a great deal of difference, too, in what a teacher can allow a class in the way of relaxation. With ninth graders, don't start joking and laughing with the class unless you intend to spend the whole period in that vein. Those younger kids just can't shift gears and get down to business when class starts off with teasing and having fun. With seniors, one of the bonuses is that one can exchange a few pleasantries, even tell a joke or two, and then turn to serious matters. They'll come with you.

Word choice is everything when you have to call a class to order. "Shut up!" is offensive. "Hush" is what I said. It has to be said daily.

Sometimes I supplemented with "You're not listening," or "Let me have your attention, please," and any other mild reminder I could think of. Calling the names of two or three talkers is effective. Asking a question of someone who isn't listening is a fair gambit. (It's an old trick. I remember that during my high school days I would deliberately look inattentive when I wanted desperately to have the teacher call on me. It often worked.)

Nobody seems to be teaching children any more not to yawn in people's faces. Every week I had to teach covering the mouth for a yawn. Maybe I should have written it into my lesson plans. Ditto for snapping, smacking, and popping gum in my face. Do adults really put up with these rudenesses at home? And do their children chew food the same way, gaping their mouths open at every munch? Who can stand to eat with them?

Beginning each class period with a "Good morning" or a "Good afternoon" is a pleasant method of catching students' attention. They soon come to expect your greeting. If you ever forget it, one of them will always remind you.

High school kids are fairly reasonable creatures. It often works just to tell them that such-and-such conduct is bad manners and you want it to stop. For example, some of them need to be rebuked for interrupting each other. They're especially bad about that in a situation where each has to take turns with you. If you once let an interrupter succeed in jostling someone aside to grab your attention, you reap a landslide of interruptions. They'll do it correctly if you insist.

I put note writing and note passing on a bad manners basis. Some students have to be made to see that their ignoring my class activities in favor of dealing with notes is rudeness. So is nodding off to sleep, a real problem with seniors who may be attending school part time and working the rest of their days. Some of them told me they ran short of sleep all the time. Considering what college is going to be costing them in the near future, one can only have sympathy for their need to earn money. Still, sleepers cannot be allowed in class. Once one fellow puts his head down, you have no basis for demanding anyone else's attention.

It seems to me that most kids really want to know and use good manners. If a teacher is careful not to make a youngster *feel* ill-bred, often she can convince him to make a change for the better. Just hearing the teacher say "please" and "thank you" at every opportunity is enough of a nudge for some students. Set up a courteous climate, and most of them will respond in kind. Just don't hesitate to correct the ones who don't.

CLOTHES MAKE THE MAN

Kids who were in our school district in the 1960s may remember a very good short story titled "Clothes Make the Man," a translation from French in our ninth-grade anthology. Its protagonist was Toto, a near-imbecile used as a lookout by a gang of burglars. They dressed him in a police uniform so it wouldn't look odd for him to be standing on a street corner, looking around.

As the uniform he wore impressed Toto more and more, he helped an old lady across the street, did other policeman-like acts, and finally—totally carried away—blew his police whistle when his friends, the burglars, ran out of the house.

Kids could understand Toto's reactions. They believed the way he was dressed made that much difference to him. If I asked them why, they usually said, "Because he was so dumb." I couldn't agree with them.

Those kids didn't notice it, but they were in the act of living Toto's experience. They were just then beginning to move from their neat, well-dressed images into the "anything goes" clothing and hairdos they wear nowadays.

This is not a diatribe against modern kids' clothes and hair. It is an effort to outline for teachers just beginning in the school system the recent history of dress codes and to show how fashions fit into the overall picture of today's young people, their manners, and their morals.

In 1964, girls in our school district were just past the multipetticoat styles of the 1950s. All girls wore dresses or skirts and blouses to school every day. Many of them still had the elaborate, bouffant hairdos you can still see in the 1950s movies. All boys wore their shirts tucked in. Some of them still had crew cuts. All of them wore their hair short.

All these years later, we seem to have bottomed out as far as deliberately "dressing ugly" is concerned. It's no longer an unwritten law that every girl has to wear her hair long, straight, and stringy, with a part in the middle, no matter how homely that makes her look. Work shirts and round, metal-rimmed glasses are seldom seen any more. It's rare to see a boy whose hair is so long that you can't tell which sex he is from the back—and sometimes not from the front.

There are lots of good reasons for blue jeans to have become popular. Durability and cheapness are two of them. I believe jeans are here to stay. I'm just thankful they no longer have to be torn and dirty to be really "in." Of course, today's adolescents have managed to adopt some really obnoxious new styles. For girls, I predict a ghastly rise in unnecessary cases of spinal curvature because our young cuties have to twist themselves like snakes to make sure of sporting the belly buttons their too-brief tops display.

I don't worry too much about today's boys. It seems to me that their dropped-crotch styles of today can't last too long. Waddling like a duck doesn't look like that much fun.

Teachers and administrators learned several needed lessons during those years from the 1960s until now. They found that arbitrary rules about clothes and hair couldn't be made to stick. Only on grounds of health and safety were they able to hold the dress code line. For instance, it's still an enforceable rule that all kids have to wear shoes at school.

The whole school district found that media pressure can change things. When a pesky little longhaired fellow in our district made a sufficient nuisance of himself, the newspapers took up his case and made him a hero. That and other instances broke down completely the hair code for boys.

A sidelight on that case: A teacher I know talked with the longhaired fellow's teacher after she'd seen his face pictured in the newspaper,

looking neat, his hair well combed back. "That's the first time this semester that I've seen both his eyes," she said. "That hair was hanging
completely over one of them every day of class—when he wasn't playing with it, using it to make the kids laugh, and disrupting class." The
news people apparently never found out about that.

What the kids learned these past decades may not prove so positive in its effects. Many of them learned that the simple acts of grow-
ing your hair long and dressing in certain ways can get you local, if
not national, fame and attention. They learned that one can punish
parents and irritate a whole generation with appearance alone. They
learned to manipulate parents into helping them defy school authorities. They learned that the more outrageous their dress became, the more admiration they could glean from their peers. It's a
lot easier, they found, to dress weirdly than to make one's mark aca-
demically.

Teachers learned to ignore outlandish appearance and concentrate on trying to reach the minds within. They're still doing it that
way. One of the seniors I found most likeable was a fellow with a Mo-
hawk haircut and one dangling earring. There was a pretty blonde I
used to see in the halls who wore a gold bead in her nose. I tried not
to think about how she kept it poised there—and what her nose hole
would look like when she outgrew the fad.

Lots of the kids have gone back to trying to look attractive instead
of ugly, even though their idea of what's attractive may vary widely
from a teacher's ideas. However, a whole cult exists that is still in the
"ugly" business. You may well get a queasy feeling, walking down the
hall behind some boy whose pants hang halfway down his buttocks
and who is having to waddle to disengage his knees from their low-
dangling crotch. It really takes practice to look at their tangled
spikes of jet-black, fuchsia, orange, or green hair without wincing.
Just keep telling yourself you'd feel a lot worse if you had to go home
to one of those kids.

I'm really sorry the kids won the "right" to use their appearances
to make social statements during school. I have seen good manners
go down the drain along with dress code requirements. Nothing can
convince me there's not a connection. Nowadays, not 1 kid in 10 who

bumps into you in the hall will say, "Excuse me." I'm not even sure they know the words. It's not that I think Sam Student over there went downhill in manners and morals because he had long hair; it's that I think he went downhill because *everybody* had long hair.

One day during the height of the dress code furor, I heard some kid say smugly, "You shouldn't judge by appearances" just once too often. I launched into a lecture that began, "Of *course* you should judge by appearances! That's what appearances are for. I don't have time to psychoanalyze every person I meet. I have to look at the appearance he chooses for himself and read that as his statement to the world . . ." and so on.

It seemed to me I made quite a convincing 1-minute presentation. I wound it up by saying, "After all, if you're really an enchanted prince, why would you want to look like a frog?"

A do-nothing, longhaired boy in the back said, "So somebody'd kiss me."

Well, at least he'd been paying attention.

ADOLESCENT MORES

Old Rules

Some rules of adolescent behavior never change. In my student days as much as now, tattletales were beyond the pale. Then as now, the worst scroungy bum in the room could demand, "Gimme some paper," "Gotta pen?" or any other desired item, and the kid he asked would hand it over, knowing he'd never be paid back. Then and now, a kid had to be driven to sheer desperation before he'd report any kind of outlandish behavior to the teacher, and even then he'd have to report it in secret.

A recent example: A girl finally asked me privately to move her because "that guy keeps putting his hands on me." I moved her and made certain "that guy" was surrounded in every direction by males. It was all I could do about it.

New Trends

An incredible delicacy in the matter of nose-blowing has blossomed in students sometime during the last 10 or 15 years. God knows, I should be the last one to fuss over any kind of delicacy, but I find it difficult to tolerate a kid's sniffling and snuffling a whole period because he'd rather die than be heard giving his nose one good honk. If we weren't testing and a student asked if he could step outside and blow his nose, I gladly gave permission. A box of tissues on the desk was a teaching must for me.

Another and more annoying new fad is yapping out "Bless you" every time any individual in the room coughs or sneezes. I battled this one, but I never managed to make much of a dent in my kids. Even the most aggressively atheistic or post-Christian kids in the room would argue sanctimoniously that they were merely expressing sympathy or "showing good manners," and they could not imagine how I could object to that. I suppose interrupting me in midsentence didn't count.

These kids who are interrupting class a dozen times a period by blurting out "Bless you" so punctiliously are the same ones, mind you, who barge down the hall, knocking six or seven people stem-winding, with never an "Excuse me."

It may be that the recent horrible episodes of school shootings will inspire parents to join forces with teachers and counselors and make strenuous efforts to teach kids that a code of silence should be carried just to the limits of legality and not beyond. I can't help but believe that if every kid had told of the threats and promises of destruction he'd heard, we wouldn't have lost as many hopeful young lives as we have.

RUDE, CRUDE, AND VULGAR

Just before graduation night, my seniors asked one year, "Are you coming to see us graduate?"

I said, "I'll be there, but I'm not looking forward to it."

They had expected a sentimental response. Why wasn't I looking forward to their big night?

"Because," I told them, "You're going to be rude, crude, and vulgar." They didn't want to hear that, but it's the truth. High school graduations have become endurance trials for all concerned, organized pandemonium that has to be staged in our big city's biggest arenas. The ceremonies are scheduled way before the end of school because we have so many high schools. Several graduations per day must be run back-to-back in order to accommodate all of us.

Add to these distressing facts the circumstance that our children have been spending their high school years training to be as rowdy spectators as the law allows. At rock concerts it is the style to scream, throw things, jump up and down, smoke pot, and mill around during the whole performance. At home, watching a television show, one can ignore the screen completely.

Most high school assemblies are planned with an audience of noisemakers in mind. Students are not even reprimanded these days for behavior that would have rung down the curtain on any high school presentation only a few years ago. Small wonder that the most meaningful performance of their high school careers is received by today's graduates with little dignity and less respect, and no trace of appreciation for the labors of those who plan the event.

What do the graduates do that is so bad? They smack, chomp, and blow bubbles with gum throughout the ceremony. They laugh, whistle, call across rows to each other, sail paper airplanes (made out of the programs, of course), and organize disruptive rhythmic clapping during the guest speaker's remarks.

When a student's name is called and he walks across the stage, the "walk" often is a prance, dance, or wriggle he has rehearsed ahead of time to impress his friends. One recent year each senior, shaking hands with the principal, deposited a marble in her palm. Sometimes it's something worse.

Parents and friends of the rowdies bring horrible noisemakers and blast the air as their offspring posture across the stage, completely blotting out the next few names on the list. Each little parent group tries to outshriek the last.

Recently some of these charmers managed to sneak a number of beach balls in under their robes—I suppose they bent down in place and blew them up. A showstopper in a past graduation was a balloon that was a full-sized nude figure of a woman. Don't ask me how they managed that. The game, of course, was to keep batting the balloons around and keep them out of hands of faculty and assistant principals who frantically attempted to confiscate them.

A guest speaker in these circumstances just has to pretend he thinks the students are listening. I have seen graduating students stand up in their chairs, backs to the speaker, to communicate with their friends. I was not very sorry for one politician we invited to speak at graduation. Every minute of her 10-minute speech was loaded with party politics. For once, I considered, she got the kind of audience her opportunism merited.

Little claques in the audience, blaring those ghastly horns that one hears at football games, cheer or boo as the names are called. At one graduation one of my homeroom seniors onstage jiggled across so wildly that he knocked off his cap and had to scramble for it on his knees before he could shake hands and get off. This was despite the fact that when they marched in between rows of teachers, many of my kids had whispered to me, "We'll be good."

After the event that year, students in each class who had heard my "rude, crude, and vulgar" remarks asked my opinion of their graduation. Had it been as bad as I had foretold? Of course I said there had been improvement, and truly, the fact that many of them remembered and seemed to care about that criticism does encourage me.

They did seem a bit less rowdy my last year. I believe a lot of them tried. The fact is that to behave throughout the ceremony with grace and decorum would mark a student in today's public schools as an oddball, a "weirdo." Not many students dared risk being that different. They hadn't had time to realize that along with their diplomas had come a great release: They were free at last and forever from the bondage of public school peer pressure.

Perhaps if we put some time and effort during each year on training our kids to be better audiences, we will win back some beauty and significance for the most important ceremony of their young lives.

6

DEALING WITH DIFFERENCE

THE REAL EXPERTS

Once a juvenile court judge came to speak to our faculty. His speech was interesting. His audience stayed with him from start to finish. The remark I remember still was a disclaimer he made at the beginning. "You are the only real child experts," he told us. "When a judge sees a child, it is after that child has already done something abnormally bad. It is likely that his background or his mentality, or both, are abnormal, too. The same thing is true of a psychiatrist or a psychologist who deals with children. You teachers are the only ones who see the broad spectrum of ordinary, normal young people."

Pediatricians, of course, see ordinary children who happen to have some illness or just need a checkup, but the time they spend with such children is far too little and usually too stressful to measure against a teacher's daily interchange with them. Parents see ordinary children, but in tiny numbers: their own few plus a few friends at a time. Scouts, Cubs, clubs of other kinds, and church groups don't provide the time with kids or the numbers that teachers see.

We public school teachers are indeed the only real child experts. Does a question leap to your mind as quickly as it does to mine: If I'm the only child expert, when is somebody in need of information about child behavior going to come around and consult me? Nobody ever has. I'm not holding my breath while I wait to be asked.

When a "survey" of any kind comes around where my only choice is to fill in a little bubble or to make a check mark here instead of there, I can't feel that my opinion has really been solicited. All such surveys tell me is, "This is the entire range of possible opinions on this subject. Kindly categorize yourself as the type of person who feels this way or that way. You have no other opinion."

Parents knew, when I told them a child's behavior seemed excessive to me, that I was talking from a background of many years of an average student load of 150 or more kids per year. Having known 4,000 or 5,000 kids on a daily basis for 9 months each seems to me a more impressive credential than multiple degrees in child psychology. So ask me.

THE BASIC STUDENT

School districts use different names to designate students who are mentally limited. *Basic* is one of those names. Unfortunately, the term often is also used by educators who mean *essential* or *fundamental*. For this chapter, *basic* means a student who cannot pass regular courses on his own.

Other names for courses geared for this kind of student are *correlated* and *CVAE*. None of these designations is synonymous with *special education*, a whole separate field that requires specially trained teachers. I don't know enough about special ed to include a chapter on it.

One terrible thing that keeps happening to basic courses is that kids are dumped into them not because of lack of intellect, but because they are completely obnoxious kids, real discipline problems who've failed time and again just because that is what they wanted to happen. These little sociopaths shouldn't be allowed to poison the well for the nice, mentally limited kids who need extra help to get through a course.

He Wants to Learn

A true basic student wants to learn. He's been through a lot by the time he arrives in senior high. Time and time again he's tried to understand and failed. He's had to see others around him progressing from skill to skill while he fumbles around still on Step 1. Often, his parents have worked with him, sometimes helpfully, sometimes frustratingly for them and him. He's found out for sure that there's something wrong with his brain. Nobody needs to tell him that, but his peers often do.

Some basic students look just like anybody else, but there is about others a distinct, dimmed look in the eyes. They need kindness. They need understanding. They soak up a sympathetic attitude like so many thirsty flowers. A teacher is in great danger of getting so emotionally involved as to forget that her aim with these young people is exactly the same as it is with regular and honors students: to teach each of them as much subject matter and as many skills as she possibly can.

Teachers have to learn what doctors and nurses do: There is a point beyond which one shouldn't get involved with the patient or the student. You're not doing a kid a favor if you're so empathetic that you can't put an F on a paper when he's earned one.

Things to expect with a basic class are short attention spans, lack of homework, chronic forgetting (books, paper, pens, anything they're asked to bring), quick irritability (mostly displayed between kids instead of directed toward the teacher), and spurts of outrageous behavior.

Keep It Short

All of a teacher's planning for basic classes should feature shortness. There should be short assignments, short seat-work exercises, short drills, short explanations. Any writing that basic kids do should be short. If you give a 25-word spelling test to a regular class, make it 10 words for basics. Instead of one or two activities planned for the 55-minute period, make it three or four short things. Even the words you use to explain things should be short.

They Don't Do Homework

That's a fact, but you're still stuck with making lesson plans that call for daily homework assignments. Even if it regularly happens that only 3 or 4 of your class of 23 basics do their homework, you aren't going to get any administrator who reviews your lesson plans, and evaluates you partly on that basis, to forgive you for not writing down an assignment most days of each week.

So write down an assignment for most days of each week! For instance, assign a two-page story in the literature anthology to be read. Then when they come to class not having read it, go over it again with them. After all, repetition is a recognized teaching tool. As a bonus to those three or four kids who actually do their homework, take it up now and then. Even grade it now and then, if you have enough other grades so you won't be failing nine tenths of the class. Or just give that grade to the faithful ones as an extra. There are many small, personal ways to show those who do their homework that you appreciate them. When you get a chance, write "I'm proud of you" under a grade. You'll make somebody's day.

"I Forgot"

Sometimes you can cut down on their forgetting to bring textbooks by refusing to let students without books take part in a class activity. Of course, the minute you tell that kid he can't participate, he starts looking for trouble to get into. You have to decide whether it's better to have to watch him every minute or to let him share with someone else. There's no need to react the same way every day. They've probably completely forgotten what you did last time.

As for other forgettings, like paper and pen, I made it as hard on the kid as I could. I refused to accept pencil work. They got a zero. A kid who's worried enough about getting a zero will either remember his materials or make sure he has a supplier in class. As for their "bumming" paper and writing materials from each other, I didn't try to stop it. That's been going on longer than I have, and I suppose it always will.

Short Fuses

Given the chronic frustrations the basic kid has to encounter, we shouldn't be surprised that he is often quick to lose his temper. There are lots of little spats in a basic classroom and, most of the time, they are over as soon as they start. If a teacher can keep her own temper and maintain an air of impartiality, she can usually soothe the kids down and resume the lesson with little harm done. I let a lot of disrespectful or even cruel jibs go past "unheard" in a basic classroom, when I would have hauled a kid over the coals for that kind of behavior in a regular class.

Even an all-out temper tantrum, with the kid screaming the worst abuse he can think of, should be met with calm detachment. Such an episode can be shattering to the teacher's nerves, but the kids don't need to know that. If the kid can't get hold of himself in the classroom, he must be sent to the assistant principal. If your hand-writing on the discipline card is shaky, no doubt the AP sees many cards written under the same trying circumstances.

If the kid refuses to go (this is truly rare), send some other kid with a note for the assistant principal to come to your room. If you have a regular insurrection or don't wish to make some other student in the group feel like a fink for carrying the message, borrow a messenger from your nearest neighbor. She'll understand.

Once the disturber is out of the room, the subject should be changed and the lesson resumed as quickly as possible. Kids will re-member it against you later if you discuss one of them after he's sent out of the room.

Once I had a student called Ned in a first-period basic class. He showed up about four times in 8 weeks. I'd noticed he used to sneak his grammar book under a stack of folders that lay on a deep win-dowsill near his desk. That way, he didn't have to remember it when he did decide to come to class.

Finally, Ned showed up in my fifth-period class one day with a checkout sheet. Not apologizing for interrupting my class, he pre-sented the sheet and demanded his book, which had disappeared from under the folders. I told Ned the truth. I had no idea where his book was and I was listing it as one that he owed to me until he found it.

Ned shouted that his book had been in the room all the time, that I must have taken it, that I must know where it was. Finally he yelled, "I want my fucking book!"

I handed back his unsigned sheet and told him to see how fast he could get out the door. He stomped out, muttering. A football player who sat on the front row said to me quietly, "Never mind, ma'am. I'm gonna get some of my friends, and we'll go rough him up for you."

It was all I could do to persuade Carlyle that I really didn't want him and his friends to beat up the foul-mouthed boy. In their code, Ned's language was a direct insult to me. Carlyle came by my room two or three times in the next day or so to see if I had changed my mind. He may have had his mental limitations, but his heart was always in the right place.

THE HONORS STUDENT

I know teachers who wouldn't take honors classes on a bet. I also know teachers who would feel insulted if they didn't get all honors classes. There are good reasons for both attitudes.

Every time we have an occasion where the public is invited, most of the parents of students in honors classes will show up. Most of the parents of students in regular or basic classes won't show up. Fewer basic parents than regular parents will show. Of course, this is why many honors students are in those higher level classes. Their parents are directly involved, constantly aware of what is going on at school. They care enough to be there. Many of them are very busy professional people, but they find time to come.

This heavy parental involvement with the brightest kids goes beyond what is useful. Usually it was fun and interesting to meet the parents of honors students, but I seldom needed to see them. I needed to see the parents of basic and regular kids. Those were the kids who could be sliding downhill and still stay in my class because there was no place to put them where they could do better. If honors students make low grades, they can be removed to regular classes.

One teacher who had refused honors classes all through her career told me that she tried teaching Major Works classes once. "All they care about is the grade," she complained. "They're not any more interested in *learning* than the dumbest kid I ever taught. They just want that A and to keep Mama and Daddy off their backs."

Her statement was only partly true, but certainly honors students can pester you to death over every grade. If you get one or more honors classes, be certain you can defend every single mark. When it comes to subjective grades like the B or C you might give a piece of prose composition (that's if your district still allows nonnumerical grading), but you should be prepared for rage, pouting, tears, and pleadings.

You need to write enough criticism on the paper to justify whatever grade you give. You can't afford to back down just once for one individual. All the rest of the class will be watching and will know exactly how the argument went, especially if you are defeated. You'll have the rest of them down on you like a ton of bricks, demanding grade changes.

These kids do homework. They have to. Any honors English class is heavy on the literature, and there simply isn't time to do the reading in class. The ones who won't read can and must be removed.

In this age of underdeveloped imaginations, many bright kids have learned to be only "book smart." Just give such a kid a book, tell him what pages to study, and he'll gladly regurgitate the material for you on tests—if necessary, word for word. But ask him to draw some conclusions, make inferences, do some supposing—in short, ask him to *imagine*—and he becomes frustrated, nervous, irritated, hostile. To him, you're not being "fair." He gets really annoyed if you tell him there is no right and wrong to it when you ask for interpretation of literature. What are you trying to do, drive him crazy?

Let me hasten to deny that I could or would defend those teachers who tell their students "a poem means whatever the reader thinks it means." That's sheer insanity. Like any other writing, a poem means what the *poet* meant. If the writer didn't make his or her meaning clear, several possibilities arise. Maybe it's just a poor attempt at expressing his idea. Maybe it's deliberate fuzziness, an attempt to disguise a lack of coherent idea. That's fakery. Or maybe it's an interesting duality of presentation that gives the reader leeway to assign two meanings, or alternate meanings, to the writing. That's art.

If the unimaginative but bright kid gets bumped back to regular class, his parent is likely to be on the phone to the principal getting him reinstated before you know it. If the parents insist, and the kid is technically able, how can you show his folks he really isn't the honors type? Take him back and do the best you can. Parents have a lot of power.

What are wonderful are the times when you can penetrate to the kids' native intelligence, stir it up, make it work. There is no greater thrill than seeing good, bright intellects begin to glow with energy. I couldn't accomplish it every day, but I did learn some prerequisites. Here they are.

- You have to know and *have thought about* the subject matter thoroughly. This includes knowing what outstanding critics have written about it, if it's literature you are studying. Usually it is.
- The kids have to be able to see and feel your interest in what you're discussing. If they can't see why it's interesting, you need to show and tell them why, convincingly.
- They have to know the opinions they offer are going to be respected (granted they've read the material) and that nobody is going to be ridiculed, overtly or otherwise.

Once you've had a few good discussion sessions where the kids really have caught fire, enough momentum usually remains to sustain the class on a high level of mutual respect, enthusiasm for learning, and general goodwill for the whole semester.

Many honors students do care to know and to understand. They will haggle over even a small point in a piece of literature until its meaning is clear to them. Most of them have felt the true thrill of learning at some time or another. They will be delighted if you help them experience it again. They are indeed very grade conscious, but I would rather deal with that extreme than its opposite: the student who couldn't care less.

USING STUDENTS

Kids like to teach, too. It's a good idea to use their budding instructional urges when you can. Sometimes when I had said it over and over in every lucid, convincing way I could think of, and I saw that a good many kids still didn't get it, I'd ask some of the kids who did understand to explain it to the rest. Usually this occurred during grammar lessons, but the same thing can be done with the interpretation of a piece of literature.

After a test resulted in disappointing grades, I sometimes established a student who had done well in each corner of the room and assigned each student who made under, say, 75, to take a turn consulting our four experts. It is surprising, not to say deflating, to notice how readily the failing kids seem to catch on when their peers are doing the teaching.

One time I walked around and listened to see what wonderful explanations the experts in the corners were giving. I found that they were using my exact words to explain, were telling the students a lot less than I did, and were liberally sprinkling their explanations with comments like "See *now*, stupid?"

Never mind; it worked.

Dangling Who?

It's easy to overestimate student instructors. Once I confronted a Major Works class with the news that the day had arrived to begin studying verbals. "You're all smart enough to take this grammar home and learn about them for yourselves," I told them, "and that's what I expect you to do. These two rows will learn all there is to know about gerunds and come back Thursday ready to explain them to the class. These two rows take infinitives. These two, participles."

We got through gerunds rather nicely, I thought. I sat in the back and interrupted only when necessary. At the end of the kids' presentation I added a wrap-up comment or two. Then we moved on to the next day and participles.

The second speaker strode confidently to the front and said, "I'm assigned to teach you the dangling participle." That is just what he did. Surprised and not sure I'd interpreted his purpose correctly, I let him go on a while before I interrupted to explain that the dangling participle is not just a special kind that one learns along with the others, but a mistake to be avoided.

I would have liked to have stopped the whole assignment at that point, but that would have wounded a lot of feelings and left out a number of students who were well prepared and who did a good job. We finished participles and went over infinitives before I took over instruction again. That was my first and last experiment with letting kids present brand-new material.

Not Expendable

If we're going to assert our rights to have students present and on time daily in our classes, we must be careful not to abuse their availability ourselves. I've known of teachers who sent each other jolly messages just to relieve the tedium, using student runners from their classes. Sometimes a teacher will dispatch a kid to the office to make some enquiry that she could make for herself later, or to fetch supplies she doesn't really need at that moment. Run your own errands, is my advice. If you're fresh out of rubber bands or paper clips, do without until you can go get them.

Sheer Abuse

Worse, in fact unforgivable, is using kids in your class to handle grades in any form: grade cards, grade sheets, notes to other teachers or to counselors about grades. (An exception: There are situations that make it necessary to send a student to the counselor or to another teacher about his *own* grade.)

I have known of teachers who handed over their grade books to trusted students and asked them to copy the grades onto the grade sheets or cards. This is unacceptable. Grade sheets merit concentration. They should always be done during the off period or at home. They should never be done by someone other than the teacher who is responsible for their accuracy.

It is a pretty widespread practice for teachers to let kids check attendance during some, if not all, periods of the day. It isn't a smart thing to do. Sooner or later, some situation will arise that will make you regret taking that little shortcut. It really is not worth the small amount of your time this practice saves. Use your seating chart!

I have heard of teachers who, finding a student on their hands who really cannot do the work, will use him to clean desks, fix blinds, or work on bulletin boards. Perhaps this is a good idea, especially if the kid is eager to be useful. What worries me is, how does one reward his work? I hope not with a passing grade for work he did not do.

There is value in helping a child feel useful, but to pretend he is successful in your class work is a cruelty whose sting will catch up with him later.

MAMA'S BABIES

Once a young, newly divorced mother told me she was sorry to hear that her 15-year-old ninth-grade son was making problems with his conduct. She was aware, she said, that he smoked pot, but she had not been able to do anything about that, either. "I just told him, he's old enough now to manage his own affairs. There's nothing I can do about it. He's on his own." Shucking off parental responsibilities isn't that easy. Most parents know that.

Every parent of a teenage student probably feels like giving up on him or her at times. Most parents hang on through high school graduation. Some are amazingly tenacious, showing up at every parent conference day or open house right through their kids' twelfth-grade years. I've seen more good than bad consequences of such perseverance. However, constant visits to a child's school are a virtue that can be overdone to the kid's disadvantage.

Some kids in honors classes, we all realize, would not be there if it were not for the constant pressure of Papa or Mama, or both. We see cases every year where students are kept in such classes even when they have demonstrated genuine lack of interest or ability, just because their parents won't hear of their dropping back to regular classes.

At the other extreme, some parents of children who belong in special education classes won't let their kids be placed there. They can't accept the idea that their children are below regular class level mentally, possibly permanently.

In spite of these misguided uses of parental pressure, I have seen enough beneficial results of close monitoring to believe most kids profit from their parents' zeal. Time and time again, students who just did scrape through with lots of parent pushing come back to visit. As a rule, they do much better in college than they ever did in high school. Those hard years of keeping tabs and insisting on performance pay off at last, when the kids mature enough to take over with self-discipline.

Lying on Demand

I'd estimate that 95% of parents nowadays lie for their kids on demand. Most of this is in the form of writing excuses for missed classes, but there are also lies about homework. Famous in one school where I taught was the parent's note explaining that the student had been absent "because of a death." Struck by the odd wording, the teacher investigated and learned that it was the anticipated death of a deer that caused the hunter's son to miss school.

Write this down somewhere in case you forget it: Unrealistic policies cannot be enforced. As long as a school district insists that excused absences will only be granted for illness of the student himself or a death in the immediate family, parents and kids will lie and cheat their way around the rules—and so will school administrators when it comes to having to enforce the unrealistic policy.

There isn't anything a teacher can do about lies parents tell. Sometimes I was glad I taught seniors just because at least I had the satisfaction of knowing that next year, Mama was going to have quite a time trying to lie her hypochondriac child through English class in college.

The Personal Touch

Some mama's babies need to have direct verbal contact with a teacher many times a week. I remember one very bright boy from years ago. If I said, "Please take out a piece of notebook paper" to the class, John's hand shot up instantly. He'd say, "Do you want *me* to take out notebook paper?" or maybe, "Do you want us to take it out of the notebook?" As soon as he'd acquired 100% of my attention, he was all right. The paper he then turned in usually had more right answers than most of the others' papers did.

Often a mama's baby will get to class early or stay a moment after the bell so that the reassuring contact will be more private. I was happy to give these quiet yearners that small amount of extra attention they needed. Most of them grow out of it little by little.

NOBODY'S EQUAL

One of the lingering 1960s notions I'd most like to put to rest is the kids' pet saying, "We're all equal." Another expression of the same fallacy is, "Everybody's as good as everybody else." These pronouncements lead directly to "My opinion is as good as anybody else's"—usually referring to some piece of literature the kid hasn't even read, much less understood.

Some students are convinced these egalitarian ideas came from our founding fathers, who did indeed say they believed that "all men are created equal." I tried to convince my kids that the founding fathers would have been the last people in the world to take their own statement as the literal truth. What they were trying to express was simply that all men have *equal rights* from birth and that nobody is born morally or politically better than anyone else.

Given a semester's time to work on it, I usually managed to convince most of the kids that they had to earn the right to opinions about literature by first reading and understanding it. Some of them even came to understand that the literary opinions of a teacher who has college degrees and decades of reading experience are more valuable than the literary opinions of a 17-year-old who hasn't read the book but has seen the movie.

Maybe I shouldn't complain. The second-rate morality that students bring to school today at least *is* morality. In the later 1960s, it was "let it all hang out" and "whatever turns you on"—and no morals about it.

It is important to remember that values are not born into anybody. They are built, a little at a time, mostly in the middle school and high school years of life. We shouldn't despair of the kids who seem to place more importance on having a good time next Saturday than on learning enough to succeed in the next decade. They won't always have such short-term ambitions. What they need from us are constant reminders that there is a future coming and that they need to get ready for it. When it comes, they'll find out how "equal" they are.

NOTICING

In a high school that has 2,500 or more students, it's hard for a kid to get noticed. Only the brilliant and the beautiful and the very, very bad can be sure of getting widespread recognition. That's why it's so important for all of us who teach to seize every chance we get to let the kids know we see them as individuals and care about them.

I made it a policy to write "Excellent" under the 100 that I put on a paper. The only times I didn't were when I had so many 100s in a batch that I knew the assignment was too easy or that widespread cheating had occurred. Many times a lesser grade deserves recognition if it is a distinct improvement. If a failing kid finally passes a test or a C student rises to an A or a B, it's fun to write "Good for you!" or "Much better!" on his paper.

Slipping grades deserve comment, too. Once in a while a kid I expected to do well would bomb a quiz or a test. I wrote, "What happened?" or some such thing so he'd know I cared. More often than not, that student made it a point to come and tell me what happened, thereby giving me the opportunity to throw in a few encouraging words about next time.

I'll never forget the time that a really slow girl who was struggling along in regular English I class stepped into my room after school. I had just graded her test. "Linda, you passed the test," I told her. "Look, you made a 70." Linda danced her way around the room, crying, "I passed! I passed!" When she stopped, she had tears in her eyes, which was just as well. That way, she couldn't see that I did, too.

Sometimes the oddest gifts or special areas of knowledge can win a kid some much-needed admiration. A quiet boy I knew, one of those tiny ones who get their growth very late, turned out to be a zodiac expert. At our end-of-the-year journalism party where everyone was supposed to reveal some hidden talent, he made a hit analyzing everyone's character according to birth signs.

Two boys, both scholarly types I had seldom heard from during the year, finally revealed during the spring semester that they were competing poets. They couldn't have told me separately, but when each discovered the other liked to write poems, that made it all right. They used to come in occasionally for a session of criticism.

Do teachers crave recognition, too? One Christmas a reserved little girl gave me a holiday greeting card on which she had written a line in Hebrew. I asked her what it said. A little embarrassed, she murmured, "I see the God in you." I have feasted on that in my heart ever since.

SOMETIMES IT'S FUN

Every so often a really good discussion would get started, usually after we'd read a piece of literature. One sees kids thinking about concepts that haven't dawned on them before, putting ideas together and discovering structures and relationships they've never noticed till now. That is one of the rewards of teaching. Another is getting to work with students on something they really wanted to do. For me, for years this was the Christmas program.

For a junior high (middle school hadn't made it to our district yet), we put on quite an elaborate show. All the music was provided by our excellent choral groups. The second half of the program featured tableaux of shepherds, wise men, and the Holy Family.

The first, more secular half consisted of everybody's favorite Christmas songs, each featuring different groups of costumed dancers and different stage sets. After each number we used a blackout to enable one group of dancers to run off and the next group to get into position. Timing was crucial.

With teacher friends, I did everything from script writing to making up faces and drilling dancers. During performances I divided my time between the spotlight crew at the back of the auditorium and an area backstage where I could help the gym teacher get dancers on and off. One year we had a darling group of six especially tiny seventh graders, dressed in feet-in pajamas, dancing to "Up on the Housetop." One little boy was so cute "you could eat him with a spoon," as a colleague remarked to me.

At the opening performance (for a seventh- and eighth-grade audience), the "Housetop" number went splendidly. In the blackout the dancers ran off. Close to me, the little boy stopped and lifted his head, struck by the applause. An expression of triumphant modesty spread over his face. He turned to an imagined audience, spread his arms lovingly, and swept into a graceful bow. "*Thank* you very much," he murmured to right and then to left. "*Thank* you very much." His bow perfected, he turned to march back onstage and deliver it!

Tears ran down my face because I was laughing so hard. I just managed to catch his little blue-pajama-clad body by the waist and hand him down the backstage stairs to the gym teacher. We had managed to stifle the youngster's stage craving for the moment, but I am sure that boy grew up to be a performer. He had heard the call of the sirens.

Of course, it's the disasters during performances that one remembers best. Talk about learning experiences! I have learned to drape a sheet or a length of material around an adolescent boy to produce a respectable-looking shepherd or a Joseph. An 18-inch scrap of tinsel makes a sparkling crown for a forgetful Wise Man. A paper-wrapped soft drink can or bottle makes a credible container for frankincense or myrrh.

When do teachers put on a Chinese fire drill behind drawn curtains while two gymnastic elves wait for their cue? Simple. When someone belatedly notices we have the gymnasts' mats upside down all across the stage just 3 minutes before the curtain rises on their number. How can a Santa Claus mess up a three-word performance when the words are simply "Ho, ho, ho"? Easy. His pants fall down.

Kids who are performing are at their best: dedicated, earnest, eager. Working with them on projects they want so much to do well is not only uplifting for the teacher, it is also eye-opening. One gets a glimpse of the kinds of effort kids can and will expend when they really care.

7

FOSTERING
FRIENDSHIPS

TAKING CLASSES

Sooner or later, you find yourself taking a class for some other teacher. This may be a personal favor you're doing for a friend or an office directive. If it's the latter, you need to make sure the secretary or whoever in the office made the assignment gives you credit for the extra work, so that you won't get called on more times than other people do. If it's a personal favor for a friend, you need to make sure the friend has official permission for his or her absence from class. Otherwise, both of you could wind up in trouble.

Certain standards should be met by both teachers, the one who is leaving and the one who is filling in. The leaving teacher should make it as easy on the substitute as possible, preferably arranging for the kids to be busy the whole time so the substitute has nothing to do but maintain order. She should also furnish a seating chart so the incoming teacher can identify any kid who decides to become a problem.

An incoming teacher should accept the assignment with at least a show of goodwill. You never know when that particular shoe will be on the other foot. She should try to answer the kids' questions, perhaps calling on others in the class for help. She should not be so preoccupied with whatever work she brought along as to let class discipline go to pot. If any students behave so badly that the regular teacher needs to know about it, the sub should make every effort to get names and facts straight and to leave a note giving the details. Better: Put it in her box.

One of the curses of having first period off is that one gets called on frequently for teachers who are running late. In those cases, it's often impossible to get a lesson started because the regular teacher hasn't planned to be absent and hasn't left instructions for a substitute. Of course, every teacher is supposed to leave lesson plans in a specified desk drawer, but often the plan may say, "go over homework" or "introduce poetry unit" or some such thing, perfectly clear to the regular teacher, but impossible for the pinch-hitter to know where to begin.

As every regular substitute teacher knows, kids believe subs were invented for students to practice mischief on. They'll sit in each other's places, answer to other kids' names, beg permits for the library, the restroom, the office, the telephone. They'll attempt every old student scam they know and try to invent new ones.

Much of this illicit enterprise can be avoided simply by making sure the students are aware that you are a regular teacher in that school, simply taking a class as a favor. They realize that even if you don't know them yet, you could well meet them later, and that you just might have a long memory for dirty tricks. Some of them will still try to put something over on you, but your odds are better if they know you're a permanent fixture on campus.

If you find no lesson plan, you might start by asking some reliable-looking kid what the assignment was or what the class has been working on. Then if it's something they can continue silently, by all means get them started on it. If there's simply nothing you can tell them to do, you can ask them to sit quietly and do anything they want, from cleaning out notebooks to snoozing, so long as it doesn't make a disturbance. If you can find the class cards, you should at least check the roll.

A good trick for any teacher is to have one or two never-fail lesson plans in a folder to be used anytime she has to miss school unexpectedly. I try to keep a writing assignment plan available and a grammar lesson one as well. If the kids are carrying their grammar books, the sub can use that lesson. If not, the writing assignment will see her through. Both plans should be detailed and easy to follow.

No matter how conscientious one tries to be, anyone can be caught short sometime. I remember one year when I was about to start eighth-grade classes reading a play in our anthology—*The Diary of Anne Frank*. Never dreaming I'd have an emergency and be absent, I'd jotted down on my regular plan, "Briefly summarize World War II." The sub was still in the building when I returned next day. She made me realize how ridiculous that plan sounded to a person who didn't know what I had in mind.

You may be shocked at some of the practices you see going on in some rooms where you take classes. That's the time to remember it isn't your place to criticize. That teacher gets evaluated, the same as you do. It is also not your place to tattle, even through the second-hand method of gossiping about conditions in that classroom, to other teachers.

Twice when I took classes I noticed misspelled words in directions written on the board by the teacher. Each time I quietly mentioned it later to the teacher. It wouldn't have been appropriate to have changed the spellings with the kids looking on. Another time I noticed a teacher had written several short-story titles on the board and put no quotation marks around them. My fingers itched. I wanted very much to walk up there and put in the missing quotation marks, but I managed to keep my hands to myself.

FLOATING

I never floated full-time, thank God. A floating teacher has no classroom of her own. Needed for an overload of students, she might teach, say, two of her classes in two different second-floor classrooms. Her other three classes might meet in three other locations anywhere else in the building. It depends on who has a conference period when she needs a classroom.

It's an inconvenience to have a floating teacher come into your room every day at your off period, so that you have to get all your work done in the lounge or the library. Think how much worse it is to be the floating teacher! Her biggest headache is the lack of storage space, especially for textbooks and resource materials. The second biggest problem is the lack of blackboard space. She can never write anything on the board and expect it to be there the next day.

A floating teacher needs to be on excellent terms with the office staff. If they sympathize with her difficulties, they can help by letting her use telephones or even desk space at times. They can, perhaps, make it easier for her to get and store materials.

Most of the teachers into whose rooms she floats will be sympathetic, even if her presence crowds and inconveniences them. Most will hand over a share of blackboard space, maybe a file drawer or two, even a bit of desk space. The floater needs to be very careful not to be messy and to keep her kids from making any problems for the room's regular occupant. If the floater and the regular occupant are still friends at the end of the year, it speaks highly of both of them. They're probably both generous and thoughtful individuals.

Administrators hate making teachers float. They have some idea of how frustrating it is to teach with no home base. If a teacher finds herself floating for the second year in a row, it's time to protest. No other teaching situation is quite so bad, and the burden should be passed around. It may be that in the press of other concerns, the administrators just forgot to make a change. Time to be the squeaking wheel.

Special care must be taken when a floating teacher orders textbooks. She should send students for them early in the period so that she can be sure of getting them issued and properly signed for during that one period. If she does have leftover books, they must be locked away, even if she has to beg for temporary storage in a neighboring teacher's cabinet. (The regular occupant of the room you are in won't be there to ask when you need her; she's working in the lounge because you are using her room.)

If you cannot get out of being a floating teacher, try using your hardship to win a special concession or two from the office. Perhaps you could get out of having a homeroom. That would save you considerable time and paperwork. Maybe you could avoid being assigned a tutorial. What do you have to lose?

GETTING ALONG WITH THE STAFF

A school is always called "the building" or "my building" by its teachers, though most schools in our district include numerous separate structures. One tends to think of the various spheres of influence in a building as so many little independent kingdoms. A teacher needs to get along with all of them.

Attendance

A main function of the attendance department is to report daily attendance to the state, based on second-period reports from each teacher. Most attendance clerks do not feel any obligation to be at the service of a teacher who may come in wanting to know why a kid has been absent four days, or what is being done about the absences of such-and-such a kid. If you want to know, ask the kid or the parent or make friends with some student who works in attendance and who will come privately and tell you what you need to know.

Student workers call the homes of absentees and ask why the students are not in school. I've seen notations of "sprang ank" and "flew" many times because student helpers often work attendance cards, but the worst disease of the lot seems to be "N.A." Must be wildly contagious. I have from one to half a dozen out with it any given school day.

Though nosy teachers are not encouraged to come bothering attendance workers with questions, those same teachers are inextricably involved in the attendance recording process. The kid whose card reads "N.A." comes back to me, not the attendance office, with a written excuse that he has been sick in bed all day. There is no good process for pursuing the matter. If I have time, I ask the student why no one answered the phone if he was there the whole time, including when the attendance office called. Then he tells me he was too sick to answer, or asleep, or in the bathroom, or anything else he wants. I have neither the time nor the clerical help to inquire further.

In one case, I called a working mother at her office at her request. Our talk confirmed her fear that her daughter had received an unsatisfactory notice that never got home. When I also mentioned her daughter's many absences, including one that day, her mother told me that the daughter had a habit of skipping school. "I can tell you where she is. She's home sleeping right now," the mother said. "I'm sure she is. She's pulled this before."

Next day, the daughter handed me a note written and signed by the mother, saying the daughter had been absent for a medical appointment. It was really the mother's signature. I checked. There was no further step I could take.

Another girl had over 24 absences during the spring semester. Back she'd pop after a day's absence, healthy as one could wish, with a note from Mama saying the girl had been ill. I tried with that one. I asked her what was the nature of the illness that would cause her to be sick one day and well the next, for more than 20 different days. She said all of her absences were excused and it made her unhappy to discuss the matter!

There is some kind of referral process that can be invoked to bring a truant officer into the case, but it is seldom used. I've also heard that a school can sue parents to force them to get the child to school or pay a fine. That, too, is seldom used. I don't know why. It seems like a procedure that would more than pay for itself.

The attendance office usually is also responsible for handling student checkouts from school. If the student is checked out involuntarily for nonattendance or something like that, very likely his books will be missing. A teacher should keep very careful records of such checkouts. She should also make a note of it if later the student's book is found and turned in. She is financially responsible for each book for which she cannot account, but, of course, if a student goes AWOL and the records show no books were turned in, the teacher doesn't pay. A good idea is to make these notes by that student's name in the grade book. You won't be using that line for any more grades, anyway.

School Secretary

A school secretary wears many hats. She dispenses supplies to teachers, from paper clips to manila folders. She hands out paychecks. She arranges for a substitute when a teacher is absent. She is usually in charge of the school calendar, arranging matters so that big events don't conflict with each other, making sure the auditorium doesn't get booked for overlapping occasions. She keeps the principal's schedule straight and screens his or her calls and callers. Teachers rely heavily on a good school secretary. She can tell them everything from when the PTA meets next to whether this is a good day for a talk with the boss. If her temperament seems a bit chancy, ask yourself how yours would be if you had to deal with 100 or more teachers every day.

Data Clerk

Usually, there is one clerk in charge of grade sheets. Her job is to hand them out to teachers, receive the finished products, check them for errors and omissions, and deliver them Downtown. It is extremely important to hand in neatly done, very accurate grade sheets on time, even if you have to sit up till all hours the night before to finish them. Data clerks deeply appreciate teachers who take pains to get their grade sheets right. Everybody from the principal down gets fussed at if there are a lot of errors on the sheets, which thereby cause trouble with the computers at the main administration building.

Registrar

This person has the final say as to who gets credit for a course. He or she also receives grades for students who transfer in from afar. Every registrar I have known has been great help with new students or with any kind of grades complication. Hers is a highly responsible position. If you lack grades for a new student and know it before grade sheet time, try to get to the registrar with your query early so she won't have a lot of teachers ganging up on her at the last minute.

Assistant Principal

The only reason I can imagine for anyone's consenting to be an assistant principal is that that is the only way to become a principal.

Assistant principals in a school have all the discipline responsibilities. They work with the security guard. They are on call for emergencies. They have charge of issuing and taking up books and of keeping track of the school's inventory.

They also get to evaluate teachers. Since our state legislature mandated annual evaluation of each teacher, including at least two assessment visits of more than half an hour each, I sometimes wondered how any of the administrators do anything else.

Principal

If any human being who deals with the public is a more constant and vulnerable target than a high school principal, I don't know who it is. Parents, students, teachers, and staff all look to the principal to make things right. It's a killer job.

My first principal thrived on stress. She ran a good junior high school and kept it staffed with top-notch teachers. I don't know how she managed. She'd give contradictory orders, get overexcited, grab the hand mike on her desk and yell for teachers, repeating the calls before they could possibly get to the office. Still, when whatever caused the crisis was over, it had been resolved her way. It's a gift.

School Nurse

School nurses try to let teachers know if a student has an unusual or disruptive physical or mental condition. Usually, a confidential memo is sent around for each of the student's teachers to initial. However, slipups do occur. Sometimes, secretive or overly proud parents prevent really needed information from getting to the teachers. It was not uncommon for me to discover that a kid who'd given me fits off and on all year had been under psychiatric care the whole time. If you have lots of trouble with one kid, try checking in with the clinic.

The nurse never asked much of me, so when she did want something, I tried to respond graciously. She has to keep up-to-date immunization records. She must rely on homeroom teachers to follow through by getting kids to take home notices of shots and boosters due. Your cooperation is important. If the kids procrastinate too long, they have to be kept out of school until they get their medical requirements met.

Once in a while the nurse interrupts a class long enough to get mass testing done for vision, hearing, scoliosis, or some such thing. Grin and bear it. Such interruptions are worthwhile.

Academic Dean

This is a fairly new category of administrator in our district. This person spends the majority of school time doing jobs like scheduling classes and teachers and organizing the tutorials program. By the way, when teachers in a building refer to "the program," they usually mean the overall plan of classes, teachers, and class periods. Putting the whole thing together is known as "writing the program," an activity that, like infinity, is beyond my imagination.

Maintenance Staff

Most school maintenance workers I have met have been helpful, agreeable, and accustomed to hard work. In a district as big as ours, however, a school's own maintenance crew is not allowed to do certain jobs. For example, the replacing of broken windows is a Downtown function. Such a job must be requisitioned and waited for until the powers-that-be get around to sending out people to do it. When they finally arrive, these workers, too, are usually easy to get along with.

Maids and janitors in a school know lots of useful information, such as where there may be unused filing cabinets or tables or desks that are in better shape than the ones you have. They are also good at getting out ink stains and replacing lost screws for desktops. Ask them.

Counselors

People usually become school counselors because they feel special sympathy for and interest in young people. A teacher who wants to get involved more deeply with kids' problems puts time and trouble into getting a counselor's certificate. Sadly, she often discovers that as a counselor she is spending more time testing youngsters than advising them. She has more conversations with the computer than with the kids.

In most schools, kids in your homeroom will stay under the aegis of the same counselor for their four high school years. This arrangement offers student and counselor the maximum number of opportunities for learning and understanding each other. As your homeroom people become familiar with their counselor, some of them want to drop in on him or her at will to discuss their scheduling or career problems. It's up to you as homeroom teacher to keep unexpected callers off a counselor's neck.

Look at it this way: If homeroom is just 10 minutes long, the kid will use up half that time just getting to the counselor's office. Then he probably has to wait to be seen. If you give him a permit to leave homeroom to see the counselor, you are really excusing him from whatever class he attends following homeroom. You have no right to make that decision for whoever teaches him next.

Right Now

Insist to any student who wants to go see the counselor "right now" that instead he must write the counselor a note specifying the problem and the student's schedule. You deliver the note at lunch or at your off period. The counselor then can send for the student at a time that will be least disruptive for all concerned.

Proctors

Counselors are in charge of all those standardized tests with which we have been swamped in recent years. Teachers have to serve as proctors for those tests in most cases. It's a task everybody despises. Usually tight security is required, so that test booklets have to be signed in and out, with many teachers lined up, waiting their turns, while one or two counselors painstakingly check their materials. Try to remember it is the process that irritates, not necessarily the counselor in charge of it.

Failures

One bone of contention between teachers and counselors is calling students who have failed a course. Even when unsatisfactory notices have been handed out and the individual may have been warned repeatedly during the semester, if he really does fail, someone (at my school, at least) has to make sure the student fills out a form specifying what he intends to do about the failure: repeat in fall, repeat in spring, forget the course, or take summer school. Counselors use those forms in scheduling next semester.

Our rule was that homeroom teachers rather than subject teachers get those forms filled out or (after a student's last exam, when he can't be located on campus to be asked about it) call his home and get a verbal commitment. Of course, if the failure does surprise a parent and he wants to know why it happened, the homeroom teacher doesn't have any idea.

From the teacher's point of view, calling as a homeroom teacher rather than as the subject teacher has its advantages. It keeps down arguments with angry parents. From a parent's point of view, it must be maddening to keep getting "I don't know anything about it" when you want to know why your kid failed. I always contended that the counselor is the logical one to make those failure calls, but I didn't expect to win the argument, and I never did.

NEIGHBORS

There is little difference in being a good neighbor at school and in being one in your home community. Tolerance and goodwill are vital in both situations. Chronic borrowing and chronic complaining are as obnoxious in a next-door teacher as they are in a next-door housewife.

You will probably develop lasting affection for the teacher next door. You go through so much together: crazy mixed-up fire drills, power outages, bad weather situations, student tears, triumphs, and tragedies. You take turns reminding each other to turn in reports, go to meetings, or do paperwork. You lend or borrow class report slips, attendance slips, and permits. In emergencies, you cover each other's classes for brief periods of time.

If you have a room in the main school building, it is easier to be friendly with the teacher beside you than with the teacher across the hall. This is because sound travels across the hall rather than from the same side, so a noisy class or a teacher's penetrating voice across from you can be misery. The only recourse you have is to close the doors and transoms, hoping she will realize why and make an effort to be less noisy.

Under no circumstances would I ever report a noisy teacher to the office. If the situation was intolerable, the most I would do would be to have a talk with the teacher. As I grew older, this kind of intervention became easier. Most often it was a new teacher who couldn't keep a class reasonably quiet, and a new teacher usually appreciates help offered in a tactful way, especially from one who has obviously been around a while.

APE CURE

This is a good place to mention my rock-bottom, when-all-else-has-failed-and-the-class-has-gone-wild technique. I called it "ape cure" because it should never be used except when a whole class has absolutely "gone ape." The last time I used it was about 9 years ago, when the mild-mannered substitute across from my room lost control, panicked, and came over to ask me to quiet his kids. They were creating pandemonium.

I put on my Wicked Witch of the West expression as I marched into the room. In the little pause created by the entrance of a different adult, I snapped, "See how fast you can get out paper and pen. You will write what I dictate. You will then recopy each sentence 10 times. You will put your name on your paper and turn it in for a check or a zero. Incomplete papers get a zero."

Stalking up and down aisles, I dictated each sentence a few words at a time, repeating as needed for the slower students.

1. Students who will not discipline themselves must be disciplined by other people.
2. It is basic good manners to shut your mouth when a teacher is talking to you.
3. It is stupid to waste class time in unacceptable behavior.

Does this solution sound too infantile for high school? When kids act like prekindergarten infants, it is perfectly all right to treat them like prekindergarten infants. It works. Those kids wrote the 30 sentences, turned them in, and were quiet as mice the rest of the period. Of course, one must really follow through, take up the papers, and convince the returning regular teacher to give zeroes to any who did not cooperate. If it is a class of your own, don't weaken later. If one does it thoroughly, "ape cure" never has to be repeated with the same class.

8

DOING OTHER DUTIES

HOMEROOM

It is hard to love a homeroom. Most of the things we have to do with our homeroom kids are data-gathering processes, so that from Day 1 we're on their backs to bring back those census cards, or PTA envelopes, or other kinds of letters or notices to parents that need to be signed, or immunization records.

Homeroom usually meets for only 10 minutes a day, if that often. In some schools it meets only 1 day a week. Under those circumstances, there isn't much chance to get acquainted with the kids. Then, too, speaker announcements often are made during homeroom so as not to interrupt regular classes. Certainly this makes sense, but it means shushing the kids just as they're meeting and greeting and beginning their day—or missing announcements because they *won't* shut up.

The best homeroom situation comes about if you get a ninth-grade group and train those youngsters in the way they should go. They will be quiet for announcements if you won't tolerate their talking while the speaker is on. They will bring back the take-home items if you hound them unmercifully until they develop good habits. After a while, the more intelligent among them are grateful to have a place where they can depend on hearing announcements, getting themselves together, and planning for a successful day.

I did insist that homeroom classes sit in alphabetical order. Ten minutes per day wasn't too much to ask, and it made all our paperwork so much easier. Sitting in order also makes taking the roll easier in the early days when you don't yet know the kids. Then there are the standardized tests, given by booklets that have to be taken up and alphabetized or put into numerical order daily. Another reason for the kids to spend 10 minutes a day cooperating with you.

In many schools the homeroom attendance card is the one used by the office daily to phone parents of absentees; that is the card you use if you have to record absences and tardies on report cards. Even if the absence information is written by the attendance office, it behooves the homeroom teacher to keep a close eye on the cards and make sure she has enough information to fill out the grade sheets correctly.

Letters From Home

Also important is the fact that when a kid comes back from absence, in many schools he brings the note from home to his homeroom teacher, who then makes out a permit that is supposed to be signed by all six of his subject teachers. In other schools, the note itself is carried around all day, so that each classroom teacher sees and signs it. In either case, that note from home should wind up in the files of the homeroom teacher, who should be *very* careful to keep all notes for the whole school year. Most of us throw them into the "hole" at the rear of the large, lower right-hand double drawer in the desk.

Technically, only personal illness or a death in the student's immediate family are acceptable excuses for absence in our district. Actually, many other excuses are accepted as excused absences. What they are varies from school to school and from teacher to teacher. For example, there are "court appearances"—which can be anything from the student's having to be at a divorce hearing involving his parents to the student's being on probation for some crime. Does the kid have a choice about going to court?

Many parents lie for their kids sometimes. Some parents do it regularly. After a time, every teacher gets to know her hypochondriacs:

kids who routinely give themselves a day at home, knowing their folks will write an illness permit for them on demand. The kids often are quite bright, so that making up missed work is not a problem for them. Since they regularly penalized me by making me take extra time catching them up, I returned the favor by making sure their makeups were harder than the original tests. Seemed like the least I could do.

Skipping Homeroom

Lots of kids skip homeroom but go to all their other classes on time. It is hard to do anything about this in most schools. My advice to the homeroom teacher is, be sure you have solid backing from the office before you go out on a limb about homeroom absences or tardies. My general impression is that most school offices really don't want to hear about it.

One thing you can do is to send home an unsatisfactory notice detailing dates the kids were absent or tardy to homeroom. Sometimes that will bring cooperation from the parent. Other times, you may find out it is that parent who causes the kid to be chronically late. If so, you're out of luck.

It's hard to say which grade level is most enjoyable to have for homeroom. Freshmen are confused about everything, apprehensive, and terribly slow making out the paperwork. Sophomores are blasé, noisy, and up to all kinds of attendance tricks. They're at the very worst age for discipline, perhaps because they still have so much more of high school before them that they can't see daylight ahead. They love to annoy teachers, and they think they can do that more successfully in homeroom than any other place. It behooves you to prove them wrong.

Juniors are beginning to calm down. They're having serious thoughts about the PSAT and going to college, and they're beginning to take more seriously the idea that teachers have something of value for them to learn. They can easily handle the usual homeroom paperwork. This is probably the easiest grade level to work with.

Seniors are almost like adults. Lots of them are beginning to remember their manners, to be thoughtful in little ways, to pick up on courtesy and goodwill toward the faculty. The hard parts with seniors are one's responsibilities toward getting them ready for graduation, attending the prom, and seeing that they arrive at graduation itself sound in wind and limb and complete with caps and gowns.

It is most comfortable for a teacher to start with a group and remain that group's homeroom teacher all 4 years. Knowing the kids well helps with all the little homeroom duties. School administrators mean for it to happen that way, with the same teacher carrying the same kids along all 4 years, but they always have to adjust for attrition, new faculty, and so on. In my 29 years I think I went through all 3 years of junior high twice and 4 years of senior high once. Those are the kids you will remember longest.

EXTRA HELP

It doesn't take long to deal with the question of extra help because so little of it is requested. School districts have policies on extra help. Ours required that it be offered on a regular weekly basis to students who needed or wanted it. I've forgotten how long extra help sessions were supposed to be. In 29 years I never needed to know.

A teacher can feel free to offer extra help to everyone and to urge it on those who sorely need it. So few kids respond that it is never a burden. I regularly invited all my students to come for extra help any morning. I was there early for makeups and for my own work anyway.

Tutorials

State-mandated tutorials on a regular schedule were instituted in our district a few years ago. Any student who failed any course was assigned to tutorials for that course for the next grading period. Different schools met the tutorial requirements in different ways. The reactions I've heard from students and teachers have been uniformly negative.

We suffered through different tutorial processes for a few semesters. Then one fall when we began school again, the tutorials just weren't there. I did not mention this to a soul, and I don't know of a student or teacher who did. We didn't want to know what had happened to them. That is the way failed programs disappear in my district.

Can't Be Done

You cannot legislate learning. You cannot make students pass when they don't want to pass. Most of all, you cannot make workers out of nonworkers by keeping them in classes 30 or 40 minutes longer per day. Some day the state legislature is going to have to swallow down these unpalatable facts of life. Some kids would not pass if all it took were pushing a button.

MAKEUPS

Next to grading papers, doing makeups is probably the worst part of a teacher's job. There are prescribed guidelines for makeups: A student missing class one day is supposed to have 24 hours to make up daily grades, seat work, or homework he missed. If he missed a test (each subject had an assigned test day while I taught), he should have 1 week to make it up. That rule I have never understood. If the student was present all the previous week and missed school only on Monday (English test day), wouldn't he be better off making up the test immediately upon his return on Tuesday instead of waiting a whole week and forgetting the material? With kids who saw my point, I went ahead and got the makeup done the first day they could come for it.

Makeups are supposed to be given before or after school. In practice, they are often given during class, so the student misses a second day's work to make up the first day's work. This is one of those little grafts that make teaching possible. Often a teacher needs to send the kid to another classroom to take her makeup, since she may be going over the test material with the others. This calls for discretion. She must carefully sound out the other teacher to make sure he or she is willing to be a party to this minor rule-breaking.

When my children were grown up and my carpooling days were over, I found it more convenient than it used to be to come to school early for makeups or to stay after for them. I don't know how young teachers with small children manage. They have many calls on their before-and-after time, and baby-sitting arrangements can't always be changed in a hurry. Some of them do makeups on their 30-minute lunch periods. One teacher can help a friend a great deal, sometimes, by offering to combine the other's makeups with her own. Those kinds of favors usually get paid back.

One important argument for sticking to before and after school for makeups is that having the inconvenience of coming early or staying late helps discourage some kids from playing sick, talking themselves into feeling bad on days when they are really well enough to come to school.

Come Early

If a teacher's family life allows it, a good idea is to come half an hour or more early every day. Then one has the luxury of offering kids makeup times any day of the week without upsetting one's own routine. Our district policy demanded that a teacher also offer at least one makeup afternoon a week, but chances are, with the every-morning alternative, those afternoon makeups wouldn't happen as often as twice a semester.

Procrastinators

Most maddening about makeups is that some kids just won't come. The last week of the grading period, most of them scramble for grades. Then they expect the teacher to furnish all the information. "What days was I absent?" "What did I miss?" "Is this all I need to do?" With varying success I tried to enforce a policy of having each student responsible to find out what he missed at the time he was absent, not 3 weeks later. (This is an important point to stress at Open House or whenever you encounter parents during the semester.) Students crowded my room the last few makeup days, and I wound up with a stack of last-minute papers to grade before I could begin to average. Served me right for not zapping them with zeroes when they didn't make up by the prescribed deadlines.

My system was far from perfect. It was my attempt to shift the burden onto the absentee's shoulders. At the beginning of each year I had each class write down a few guidelines (high school students think they're too old for "class rules"!), including some such wording as this concerning absences: "Before you are absent, get phone numbers from several students in this class. The day you are absent, call and find out what you missed. When you return, tell me when you are coming to make up the work. Do not ask me what you missed. I cannot interrupt class to tell you."

Of course, they would still line up at my desk upon their return, expecting to have me explain everything that happened while they were gone. I held my ground and chased them away. Teachers who do not do this will find themselves wasting the first 5 or 10 minutes of class time, catching up absentees.

In case I sound too virtuous, I'd better admit that when it's about time to send home unsatisfactory notices, I put on the board all grades the class should have in each of the three categories I use: daily, tests, and miscellaneous, which includes all oral work and written compositions. This is babying the kids, and I was not proud that I did it, but it really was necessary to cover myself to some degree in the matter of missing grades. There are too many absences, too many excuses, too many individual circumstances for any teacher to remember. A thorough checkup on grades and makeups sometime during the grading period is essential.

IN-SERVICE

In-service is a much-abused noun that often is used as a verb. An attendance clerk might say, "I in-service each new teacher about our attendance procedures." Never mind. We shall deal with the noun.

Before the kids came back to school every fall, we had a few days devoted to in-service. One's particular school took the first day.

There were faculty meetings, department meetings, grade-level department meetings. The next day used to be devoted to districtwide meetings, usually organized by subjects and grade levels. The idea was to refresh and strengthen teaching skills by having experts, mostly experienced teachers, present methods and new ideas to the teacher groups.

In a district as large and diverse as ours, a major problem with inservice is that what are good tactics in a school on one side of town simply don't apply at a school on the other side. There are hardly any generalized ideas that can be useful districtwide. Our best inservice presentations are those that pinpoint a special teaching area—say, introducing poetry in middle school—and leave it to each listener to make the ideas applicable in her teaching situation.

If you are asked to do a presentation, it will be because somebody thinks you are good at teaching. Two things to remember are that an audience of teachers *wants* to learn new things from you and that you should not aim too high. Teachers will not feel insulted, but rather grateful, to someone who gets down to a basic "this is the way I do it" presentation. If it is the same thing the listening teacher is already doing, you will have put a stamp of approval on her methods. If your ideas are new to her, she will give them serious consideration. A third big point is that teachers want lots of handouts. They really use them.

There are ways to spell out tactics in a simple manner without insulting anyone's intelligence. Do it. Remember, this audience doesn't want to be impressed with your erudition. What they crave are ideas that will work in their classrooms.

9

COPING WITH COMPLICATIONS

TOO MANY MASTERS

Teachers have too many people to please. There are the students, each individual and each class with its different needs. There are the parents, not all of them knowing or caring what goes on at school, but to a man cognizant of their rights, their children's rights, and the teacher's responsibilities. There are the active PTA members, a small but often aggressive group that proves a whole is greater than the sum of its parts.

There is the administrative staff of one's school, a group that evaluates each teacher formally and informally throughout the school year. There are the school counselors, with the faults and virtues of consumer advocates, students being their consumers.

There is Downtown. In my school system, that is what we called the central district administration. Downtown does not, in my experience, do much to help the individual teacher. Its decrees are usually of the "thou must" variety. For example, thou must take three precious end-of-semester days to administer a writing assignment designed by Downtown, laboriously graded according to Downtown's formula by a teacher who is not expected to include that grade in her records, and filed forever in case somebody from Downtown ever decides to look at it. (This was called "proficiency testing" in our district. Mercifully, in the last few years I taught, it

somehow slipped through a crack and disappeared, I hope forever.)

Even when Downtown tries to ease teachers' loads a bit, the effort
seldom is effective. An example: A teacher listening to our former
superintendent's monthly broadcast called in on the Hotline to mention that teachers are required not only to write on daily lesson
plans the ELO (Essential Learning Objective) number but also to
spell out the objective each time the number is written. The teacher
asked the superintendent if we could shorten plan-writing time by
simply putting the ELO number, since everyone concerned had
copies of those numbered ELOs.

The superintendent answered benevolently that merely writing the
ELO number would be sufficient. As soon as possible after I heard
about this (I had been irresponsible and not watched the telecast), I
mentioned it to our dean of instruction and asked her to confirm our
permission to use ELO numbers only. "We don't have this change in
writing, I'm afraid," she told me. "We'd better stick to the old way until we have written documentation of the change." Ready for this? She
never got around to asking for such written documentation.

Less often heard from, but occasionally potent, is our state legislature. Every once in a while our lawmakers come out with a whop-
per that changes our lives. No Pass, No Play, for example. This new
law's essence is that athletes who are failing cannot play in competition with other schools. In fact, no failing students can participate in
any University Interscholastic League (UIL) events.

I heartily agreed with No Pass, No Play, but I wondered if any law-
maker dreamed of the hardship it puts on individual teachers. As often as once a week, endangered athletes showered our desks with
queries from coaches who had to know who was still on the team.
We were expected to delay class while we looked up and averaged
grades for each player. As one observer remarked, "No Pass, No Play
should have been the rule all along—with *parents* enforcing it, not
the teachers!"

Another blockbuster bill was signed in recent years by our gover-
nor. It decreed no smoking on public school campuses. A reformed
smoker myself, I could imagine the hardship this was to many of my

colleagues, not to mention students who had until then depended upon designated smoking areas. If it worked to ban smoking by passing a law about it, we had better try Prohibition again.

INTERRUPTIONS

The best lesson you've planned all year can be destroyed by interruptions. Most principals are aware of this and make good efforts to keep the loudspeaker turned off during class periods, but occasionally the speaker will catch you in midsentence. Of course, it always happens just in time to kill the climax to which you were building.

Stop the Music

There is nothing a teacher can do about speaker interruptions except to pick up the pieces, backtrack if needed, and go on. I have heard of teachers who stuffed rags into the speaker box so it couldn't be heard in their rooms, but that's a dangerous game. Sooner or later, that speaker is going to say something you need to hear.

In my early teaching days, our excellent principal had the foible of snatching up the hand microphone which was (unwisely) located on her desk and issuing orders whenever something came up that excited her. She was a smoker, and agitation made her cough, so we often heard a series of hacks and huffs before she became coherent. On one memorable occasion in late May, the day arrived for lockers to be cleaned out. All the janitors and maids were assigned to bring garbage cans to various locations in the halls to collect the incredible reams of trash that kids accumulate in a school term.

During first period the principal, between coughs, announced that the maids and janitors were to bring the garbage cans to their assigned positions. We went on with our lesson. Our principal was never good at waiting. Five minutes later, she called again for the maids and janitors to bring the garbage cans. We went on with our lesson. Five minutes later she shouted furiously, "All you maids and janitors, grab your cans and get into this office!"

Something I considered important as a matter of personal integrity was to quell any snide or derogatory comments students made at the expense of whoever was doing speaker announcements. Of course, when someone makes a funny or ridiculous mistake, the kids are going to laugh. I see no harm in that, and I often laughed with them, but their making adverse comments about the speaker is a harmful thing. One can make it an opportunity to point out the unfairness of all behind-the-back remarks. This is especially effective when the announcer is their fellow student.

Situations arise wherein students try to discuss the faults of other teachers. If the teacher being criticized is one you dislike, you may feel a seductive urge to let the kids continue, but it won't do. Even if they don't think it through consciously, most kids will sense that there is something second-rate about a teacher who allows negative criticism of an absent colleague. Too, any such discussion is definitely an interruption of regular class activity. It should be squelched just for that reason.

Walk-Ins

An annoying and more frequent kind of interruption happens when messages from counselors or other administrators are brought to the classroom. A quick query or a request for an attendance card is soon disposed of, but frequently the request is to send a student to the office. Whether the kid is wanted for class changes, future program planning, or discipline, I resented his being taken out of English class. It seemed to me that counselors and assistant principals, all of whom have copies of each student's schedule, could arrange to see these kids during their gym or elective periods with far less disruptive effect than when they are snatched out of academic classrooms.

Very likely administrators would counter this argument by pointing out that the kid had to be seen at once for a variety of reasons: the parent was there, it was an emergency situation, and so on. That may be true for one interruption out of five. I maintain that the other four shouldn't happen. Don't expect to win battles about this with the administrators, but you owe it to yourself to keep trying.

Complaints from academic teachers may at least slow down this form of interruption a little.

Most student messengers simply walk in. A few knock. Some don't know they need to touch base with the teacher first, especially when the message is for one of their friends. I made sure they learned to check with me, no matter what the message was. That way, I wasn't bothered by the foolish few on any campus who would run in and out of classrooms, visiting their friends. How do these visitors get out of the classes they are supposed to be attending? Don't ask me. I know only that I've never seen a school where there weren't a few wandering students in the halls at every period of the day.

I'll Get It

If your classroom is in a "shack"—the school district prefers to call it a temporary building—the door will be closed most of the time. Most messengers just pull it open and enter, but sometimes there is a knock. If it was possible, I opened the door myself. In my consciousness, and I suppose in the minds of most teachers, were haunting memories of one or two "mad bomber" stories, and, of course, now there are the ghastly school shooting episodes. In almost 30 years such a thing never happened to me, but if some escaped lunatic or maddened student ever knocked on my door, I wanted to be the one to greet him, rather than one of the kids for whom I was responsible.

Missed It

We did have a streaker once in my junior high teaching days. He made his way upstairs, exhibited his crowning beauties at two doors, and got downstairs and clear away while the stunned teachers were trying to get word to the office. I was in another part of the building and missed the whole thing. Later, one of the teachers involved was mourning her lost opportunity. "If I'd just thought fast enough, I'd have chuckled, 'Oh, *look!*' and pointed at him with one hand while I put the other hand over my mouth to stifle my giggles."

Sending for Students

On 2 or 3 occasions, a kid came into my room without a permit and said that the assistant principal wanted to see this or that student. Don't you believe it! Assistant principals *always* send permits or at least notes when they send for a kid. Each time that a kid came to me with a verbal message only, I sent a note to the AP to check, and each time I found that the kid was just trying to get a friend out of class. Also, when a kid has been sent for, he should have a permit when he returns. *Always* insist on permits, coming and going. And remember to check an absence from class *that day*. You won't remember it a week from Wednesday.

The most damaging form of class interruption is really student interruption. A kid will show up with a permit excusing him for all or part of class "to help with the Ag show" or "to rehearse for program" or some such thing. Again, objecting won't get you far, but it will perhaps slow them down.

Kids were permitted to miss my class to bag and deliver jelly beans, to blow up balloons, to clean up after guests had been served a meal, and to decorate for future celebrations. Why is it always the kids who can least afford to miss class? I think I know. Lots of times I felt sure the kid told the sponsor, "Oh, *she* won't mind. We're not doing anything in English today." *Never* true! I mind, I mind!

Teacher to Teacher

Sometimes a kid showed up seriously late to class with a permit from another teacher, "finishing test." That shouldn't happen. If the test is a reasonable length and the kid has taken too long to finish (usually that means too long to start), I see no reason why he should be excused for it. He should have to hand in his unfinished test, or at the very least he should have to take an unexcused tardy to his next class. We aren't doing kids a favor when we let them get away with taking too much time on a test. We're preventing them from learning that in adult life unfinished work gets penalized—often by the loss of a job.

What also should not happen, and almost never did, is for a teacher to delay a student's arrival in class by talking to him. I always checked. For every 10 times a kid said, "Couldn't help it. My math (art, history, science) teacher was talking to me," I found that on 9 of those occasions the conversation was initiated by my tardy student. Often it was only a fleeting exchange.

Sometimes the kid does keep talking too long and makes himself tardy. I didn't excuse that, or any other tardy, without a permit. Once or twice I found that some too-kind teacher let herself get talked into giving a permit to a kid who made a practice of consulting other teachers when he should have been getting to class. A brief conversation between teachers usually cures that.

School-Related Absences

Every year there are a certain number of interscholastic competitions, field trips, and the like that take students out of class. While a distressingly high percentage of these interruptions are for athletic events, many of them provide valuable experiences and should be tolerated as equably as possible. However, the teacher should make sure students understand that they are excused only from class and not from class work they miss.

Fire Drill

Maybe if schools stopped having fire drills, we would miss them; anyway, they are necessary nuisances. A teacher's obligation is the same in every school I know about. She herds the kids out along a prescribed route, making sure lights are turned off and windows and doors are shut. As soon as I heard the three bells, I always sang out, "Girls, take your purses." I used to let some kid be the last one out. When I grew more distrustful with advancing years, I made myself last out and closed the door.

Three times in my teaching career the fire truck really came. In two cases there was a fire in some wastebasket or other. The third time, I heard there was some kind of explosive device that was defused before it went off. We stayed out more than an hour that time so the experts could make sure there were no more such devices around.

Every once in a while, a bomb threat is phoned in. I've heard school personnel say, "It's time to check the absentees for today." They say it is usually some kid having a "sick" day who decides to give the school a scare. When we found ourselves still outside after 10 or 15 minutes, rumors started to fly. What a comedown when the two-bell signal rang to return to class!

THE IRATE PARENT

One of the most useful pieces of advice I've ever had was given to me in the teachers' lounge early in my first year. Somebody said, "When you find yourself facing a really angry parent, start *with your mouth closed.* Let that parent talk. He or she will let off a lot of steam. Just stand there and nod and listen till the person is all through. *Then* get in your licks." It worked every time.

Susie's Neck

In one case, a tiny little lady came bouncing into my room, spitting fire. It was hard not to laugh. She was so small, I probably could have made two bites out of her. She lit into me, telling me how badly I had treated her child, what a terrible teacher I must be, how angry she was about the situation. I let her rave. When she stopped, I asked questions to get her going again. When she was finally all through, I said, "Does Susie have a sore neck?"

"*What?*"

"I was wondering if Susie has a sore neck. After our little run-in, she spent the next 40 minutes with her head twisted around—like this—so she wouldn't have to look at me. It must have been acutely uncomfortable for the child."

After a little more conversation in which I gave the mother my version of what had happened, the lady relaxed and was even ready to smile over Susie's childish reaction. We began to seek the real reasons why Susie's temper had exploded that day and in that way. The mother said Susie's home behavior over the past few months had changed. Susie was going straight home and to her room every day and staying there except for mealtimes.

After she said this behavior change had begun about 8 months before, the mother casually mentioned that she had remarried—about 8 months before. It was not my place to pursue the matter further, but I did suggest that Susie's lack of desire for friends and her apparent lack of interest in her family might be quite serious. I suggested that they seek some outside counselor. I hope they did. At any rate, Susie became her usual quiet self once more, and we didn't have any more head-on collisions.

Voulez-Vous

You'd think an old tabby like me would have ceased to be shocked at the younger generation, but sometimes they still surprise me. I was stunned when a neat, quiet little eighth-grade girl showed up wearing a T-shirt that read, "*Voulez-vous couché avec moi?*" ("Will you sleep with me tonight?"). After reflection, I stopped the girl as she was leaving class and asked her what the words meant. She said she didn't know, so I told her. I asked her not to wear that T-shirt to my class again.

I was more shocked when the girl turned up soon in the same T-shirt. I asked her again, privately, not to wear it to school. She wore it again inside of 2 weeks. I handed her an unsatisfactory notice to take home.

Both the girl's parents came to my second-floor room the next day. Mama was huffing and puffing, and first informed me that I was probably going to be guilty of causing her to have a heart attack because she had a weak heart and shouldn't climb stairs. I never found out why the two of them didn't simply stop by the office on the ground floor, explain about the stairs, and send for me.

Mama's next piece of news for me was that I lived in a tree, that all modern 13-year-old girls went around wearing written invitations to anybody who read their shirts to go to bed with them, and that their little girl hadn't had the slightest idea what her T-shirt said until I told her, thus corrupting her mind.

I didn't get very far with those two. I tried to force a little logic into their minds. For example, if the girl didn't know what the words meant the first time, how about the second and third wearings? Also, where were they when she needed to know what kind of invitation she was wearing? Also, if there was nothing wrong with the message on the shirt, why did they resent my explaining it to her? I invited them to stick around long enough to read every T-shirt that came down the hall. They wouldn't have found another one openly soliciting. (This was back in junior high school and some years ago.)

They probably didn't hear a word I said. Having told me off and put me in my place (in a tree, that is), they huffed and puffed out of there. Their 13-year-old hustler continued to wear her shirt as often as she wished. I often wonder whether she's achieved professional status yet.

Little Red Spots

Lollie was a B–C student, rather quiet, a little overweight, definitely not a discipline problem. Then came time for oral reports. That was the fancy name I gave to having my ninth graders stand up and read book reports they had written.

I introduced these reports by explaining how important it was for the students to become able to stand before an audience and present material. As usual, I pointed out some obvious pitfalls and tried to get the kids relaxed. Several of them had given their reports by the time I called on Lollie.

The child absolutely refused to give her report. So did her bosom friend. When I insisted, Lollie said it made her ill to stand in front of a class and recite. So did her bosom friend. I asked for a note from each girl's doctor and said that otherwise, each girl had a zero.

Each girl brought a doctor's note the next day. One doctor had written that "Nancy has told me it makes her nervous to give oral reports." The other doctor had written that he believed it would make

Lollie uncomfortable to give oral reports. I pointed out that there was nothing in either note that gave any medical reason for the girls' not doing the assignment. I gave each a zero. Lollie's parents phoned and set up an appointment with me.

I could see at once that Lollie's mother, a nurse, was the angry one; the father just sat back and listened. The mother ripped into me about how much Lollie had cried and how nervous I had made her. At the end of her lecture she told me that Lollie had never been able to do oral reports, and that when she tried it, she broke out in spots "all over her chest and her neck. Here and all down here—I've seen them."

I asked, "And then what?"

"What do you mean, 'and then what?'"

"After she breaks out in little red spots, then what happens?"

Mother hesitated. "Well . . . nothing."

"Do you rush her to the doctor, or what? Are there more symptoms? What do the spots do next?"

Father was seeing the point. "They go away," he said.

I set to work explaining why it seemed to me very important that Lollie's can't-do attitude should change. I made as strong a plea as I knew how for those parents not to back up her wimpy refusal to try. I promised that I knew the girl could do it. "Let's let her break out in spots," I urged. "Stand firm now and you may get rid of those spots forever."

The father won over the mother, and they reluctantly agreed to back me up and insist that Lollie make her report. She did. It was pretty bad, but I gave it as high a grade as I could for the extra effort it had cost. Lollie broke out in spots. She came and showed me one or two of them privately, but there was a gleam of victory in her eyes. She'd done the report! So had her bosom friend.

A couple of months later, Lollie came to tell me goodbye. Her folks were moving back to Florida, where they'd come from 2 years before. I grabbed both her hands. "Lollie, promise me you won't let them baby you back into being a loser, or I won't let you go!"

She promised, and we parted the best of friends. That's what happens just when you think you've won one. They move on, and you never learn the end of the story.

All three of my illustrations are about angry mothers because I seldom had a confrontation with a father who was angry with me. There are logical explanations for that. In the first place, more mothers than fathers have time to come to school and deal with teachers. In the second place, an angry father is more likely to try going over the teacher's head. He'll try to get the principal or assistant principal to reprimand the teacher.

This tactic may satisfy a paternal ego, but it is highly ineffectual. The first move that administrator is going to make is to call in the teacher and ask her side of the story. In 99 cases out of 100, the administrator is going to side with the teacher, even if he or she deems it expedient to try to placate the parent.

In all cases of dealing with parents, angry or otherwise, I urge you to reiterate this important point: You and the parent have the same goal. You are each trying to the best of your abilities to see that that child gets educated. With that common goal, you and any reasonable parent should be able to come to a meeting of minds.

Always try to remember to thank that parent for coming and to mention that just by showing up, he or she has done a significant supporting action that their child can see and appreciate. The angrier they are, the harder it is on them to make the effort. Your words of praise may be the only thanks they get.

DOGGING IT

Nobody really knows what you are doing in that classroom day in and day out except you and your students. Even with the added assessment visits, a teacher who wants to shirk responsibility can do so most of the days. She knows in advance when the assessment visit will be; she can always get up a "dog and pony show" for the evaluator and slip back into sloth the rest of the time. Some of the bad tricks I have seen through the years are discussed in this section.

Dragging In

Some teachers are chronically late to their classes. Some of these are smokers, taking a few last puffs. Sometimes they're just the garrulous ones who hate to leave good lounge listeners and go back to work. Kids get used to having them drag in anywhere from 2 to 10 minutes late. How much more time is lost before the tardy teacher can restore order and begin the day's work, I don't want to think about.

Slipping Out

Some teachers chronically slip out early, leaving a class to amuse itself for the last 6, 8, or 10 minutes. If you teach nearby, you will know when this happens by the rising noise level after the teacher has walked out. Smoking, again, accounts for a lot of these; some teachers just can't wait for the next puff. Others probably belong to that puzzling clan who dash out of *any* gathering 5 or 10 minutes early "to get ahead of the crowd." You know the ones: They will leave a tied-up ball game, a drama just before the climax, a great concert before the last movement. You'd think they attend events only in order to demonstrate that they can get out before everybody else.

During my last teaching years I was a few doors down from a teacher who made a habit of getting her students started on some sort of written exercises or composition and then simply walked down the hall to the lounge and engaged in numerous extended personal phone calls. I had second period off. If I entered the lounge at any time during that period, she was nearly always there. Naturally, at first I assumed that second period was her conference time also. I was dumbfounded when I finally realized that a classroom full of noisy, frolicking youngsters was where she was supposed to be at that hour.

Did I do anything about it when I learned that she was neglecting her job that way? Certainly not. That sort of noticing is supposed to be the job of any or all the administrators. That's what they get paid better than teachers for, so that they can monitor and make sure each teacher is doing her job. When a teacher chronically absents herself from the classroom and they don't know it, they're not doing their job.

Sitting Down on the Job

Show me a teacher who sits during an entire class period and I'll show you a teacher who is retired and doesn't know it. Sitting down at her desk, I mean. To the kids, that desk is as much an authority figure as a teacher herself. It isolates the teacher from the students. It makes, for some, an intimidating and impenetrable barrier.

Lots of us like to be closer to the kids, but we find that standing in one spot for too long is hard on the back. Walking around the room is good practice for part of the time, but sooner or later, you need to sit. A good way not to remove yourself from the students is to turn one of their desks around and sit in it, facing them. That was my favorite position for discussing and interpreting poetry and other literature.

If your room is large enough, you can place the students' desks in a double horseshoe around the room, so that you can see all the faces when you're having a discussion. My last teaching room easily accommodated this setup, and it was delightful. We used 32 desks in this formation, and they could all see me, in a student desk facing them, and the blackboard behind my teaching desk. Nobody was hidden down a row of six or eight kids.

On test days or student writing days you will probably find yourself sitting at your desk a good part of the time, but try to never spend a whole period there. Especially if you know certain kids to be untrustworthy in test situations, get up and walk to the back of the room. If you get tired of standing, bring some paperwork and sit back there for a while. Derriere off the chair, teach!

Stealing Time

Some teachers feel justified in doing paperwork or grading during a class period, leaving the kids to work silently on some assignment or to read. In maybe 5% of cases I can see a little justification, but these occurrences should be rare. Kids probably won't tell on a teacher who ignores them on a regular basis; they're getting out of a certain amount of work that way, or they're doing homework on class time and thereby lightening their own loads. Very few of them will be concerned enough about the lost learning time to realize they're being gypped.

On one of those rare occasions when someone has dumped an unexpected, must-be-done-yesterday job on you, and your ox is well and truly in the ditch, tell your students how it is. Apologize for the fact that you have to work at your desk instead of with them. Don't let them think you're going to do this as a regular thing or that you don't know any better.

SURVIVING THE BAD GUYS

When we teachers gripe about this or that condition, we usually wind up facing the fact that there's no particular individual to blame. Our textbook accounting system, for example, took many years to develop into the inefficient and burdensome hardship on teachers that it was in our district until the last few years.

Our chaotic mishmash of standardized tests "just growed"—no one person is responsible for the mess. In one respect, however, a teacher does sometimes find herself directly at the mercy of a bad individual, and there is little or nothing that teacher can do to change it. That happens when one realizes the principal of her school is an incompetent bully.

Let me hurry to add that I suppose only a minority of principals in our district merit that description. My first principal and my next-to-last one were shining examples of the opposite extreme: highly competent, amiable, effective, and gracious. The fact remains, I have both worked for and heard about the kinds of principals described in this section. Every incident described herein was either witnessed by me or told to me by an eyewitness.

A principal in a junior high school became furious because there had been repeated incidents of kids' taking a whole roll of toilet tissue or a packet of paper towels and stuffing them down the toilet to stop up the plumbing. In retaliation, he ordered all the doors removed from the cubicles in both boys' and girls' restrooms. That is the only time I know about when there was a fast, effective reaction. An area superintendent got wind of the situation through an outraged parent. She descended upon that school and the doors were replaced in 24 hours' time.

A bad principal can and will use the program to punish teachers who displease him. In one case, a teacher who had taught nothing but history for close to 30 years had an English teaching assignment suddenly dumped on her. It was not only unnecessary, it was inconvenient all around. Other English teachers had to be shifted around to make it happen. He never even told the history teacher how she had displeased him.

A principal who detested what he referred to as "the subculture" demanded that a black teacher who had been out for the customary 3 days because of her husband's death must furnish a death certificate for his inspection.

A principal used to make a speech to his faculty each fall, explaining that women wearing pants could not possibly retain the respect of their students. He therefore would not be able, he said, to "back up your discipline" if any of his women teachers elected to wear pants in spite of his warning. "Don't send to the office for help," he warned.

This no-pants rule was never relaxed, even in the case of a teacher who wore a permanent steel leg brace. On one of our once-in-a-decade snowy mornings, a gentle teacher who always dressed more elegantly than the rest of us showed up wearing a most attractive pantsuit. She went into the office to make sure the principal would approve. He did not. Although unaccustomed, like the rest of us, to driving on snowy streets, she trekked the 20 or 30 minutes' drive back home, changed, and came back in a dress.

Cool It

The principal gets to control building temperatures. I knew of one who wore wool business suits all school year and set the temperatures at so chilly a level that at least 90% of the women teachers had to wear sweaters every day. He appeared to enjoy hearing about how cold and uncomfortable the women were.

Face Him Down

One soon comes to understand the psychology underlying malicious and petty behavior such as I have described here. It becomes obvious that the administrator knows he is holding down a job that he is not smart enough to do well. His only hope of control is through fear. There's only one way to get along with this type of bully: One has to face him down. Once a situation arises that gives you the opportunity to call his bluff, he'll never trouble you directly again—except, perhaps, for giving you an ice-cold classroom and the general chill he manages to spread over the morale of the whole faculty.

Chicken-Yard Mentality

Intimidation is the name of the game of such individuals. They cover their own inadequacies by frightening subordinates away from close inspection of their job performance. Not surprisingly, they expect teachers to intimidate their students in the same way. It's a chicken-yard mentality. One good consequence of such a principal is that his faculty becomes close-knit. Teachers will become intensely loyal to each other. They need each other to survive.

In our district, there isn't anything one teacher can do about a bad principal. I have known for sure that a principal's superiors in the district knew of certain of his practices that were questionable at best. Those superiors did nothing. Maybe it's that hard to find principals. As I have said elsewhere in this book, being a principal is a killer job. If your situation is being made too intolerable by such a petty tyrant, better plan to transfer when you can.

Maybe some shifting of powers would make easier the life of the principal and those of his staff as well. There are nowadays faculty advisory committees on most campuses in our district. Judicious use of these groups might bring about better situations for all faculties. It's worth a try.

A SWARM OF MOSQUITOES

One day a small group of parents and teachers met with a school board candidate for afternoon tea. The candidate urged us to tell him about our needs, complaints, and worries. What did we spend most of the afternoon fussing about? The horrible new grade sheets we had just received.

That doesn't sound like much of a gripe for adults to have, does it? That's the trouble with teaching. Our two major complaints, inadequate pay and the fact that our jobs are 95% accountability and 5% clout, are beyond the reach of school boards to fix, and we all know that. So most of our complaints are about small matters. It's just that there are so *many* of them. Sometimes it feels like standing in a swarm of mosquitoes. No one bite amounts to much, but if you get bitten enough, you can be really sick.

New Grade Sheets

How bad can it be to have a poorly designed, hard-to-read grade sheet that calls for lots of unnecessary data? It can be very bad indeed. At the end of each grading period, a teacher has to enter (write and bubble) a grade for each student. Given the average teacher load, that is 150 grades or so. Then she has to decide in each case whether to enter a conduct cut or not. Not entering a cut means the student receives the highest conduct mark, an E. Most students get Es from most teachers most of the time. The new grade sheets then asked for entries for excused absences, unexcused absences, and tardies. Imagine the time required to look up those figures and enter and bubble them for 150 kids!

Because the griping was so vehement and so universal, the new grade sheets were modified. After that, we added up tardies (three made one absence) and entered only one attendance figure. Of course, the looking up still had to happen, even where the students had perfect attendance. The worst thing about the modified new grade sheet was that recording the exam grades had to be done *on the back* of the grade sheet, as all those other statistics had used up the front. Oh, well . . .

Extra Duties

The school where I last taught is so careful not to give extra duty assignments without some compensation that I thought I'd died and gone to heaven. I know of plenty of schools in this district, however, where teachers are regularly assigned to guard duty in the cafeteria, the parking lot, the halls, or the students' restrooms. In one case, we had rotating assignments of guarding the hall beginning 30 minutes *before the bell rang* for students to enter the building!

When I asked our area superintendent about that one, he said, "Your principal can do that as long as he distributes the assignments fairly among all the faculty members." I assured him that there was no fairness about it, that some faculty members had this duty and others did not. No answer. Nothing happened. We kept doing that pointless duty, guarding an empty hall 30 minutes per day. We were required to sign in early to do it.

Supplies

Usually, there is something to complain about with respect to supplies. Sometimes it is textbooks. There are not enough to go around, or the bookroom is hard to get to, or orders take too long to be filled. Sometimes—lots of times—it is paper. Either there is no long paper or there is no short paper, or there is no paper at all. One learns to be very crafty about hoarding a little emergency supply. Usually, there is a teacher who will trade the kind you want for the kind you have.

Since the coming of the modern copier, there is a whole new world of easy duplicating for teachers. The trouble is that copying on a new machine is a lot more expensive than on the old-fashioned duplicators. Also the modern machines, overworked as they are, tend to break down every so often. Of course, these breakdowns usually will occur right when you have really counted on getting something copied.

In some schools I know of, a teacher has to turn in her order a day or more in advance for photocopied material. Copies are made on a first-come, first-serve basis. Teachers cannot operate the machine themselves. I feel sure this rule has cut down on the number of calls to the service man.

Perennial Problems

Some of the other small annoyances that build up in teachers are matters that simply would not happen to people in other professions. For example, parents wanting a conference are supposed to call and make an appointment for the teacher's off period, but if a parent just shows up during the school day, the teacher is supposed to handle the matter tactfully, if possible giving up her needed 5 minutes between class periods or her 30-minute lunch to satisfy that father or mother. Can you imagine patients barging in on a doctor that way?

Feeling the Heat

Another little irritation is the fact that no teacher in the main building can change the temperature of his or her own room. Both heating and air conditioning are regulated from afar. Of course, teachers can open the windows—but in many buildings, the windows were sealed shut when air conditioning was installed. Also, in our climate, the heat in April, May, September, and most of October prevents anyone from opening the windows. The rest of the time, it's too cold.

Those who teach in "shacks"—more properly called temporary buildings—have an edge in the fact that when the main building air conditioning breaks down, as it does several times a year, the shack people go right on with their two window units per room. They have two heaters, too.

The only problems the shack teachers have is that the air conditioners make a continuous noise that has to be talked or read above, and the heaters are placed high on the walls. Someday, somebody is going to make our district officials understand that heat *rises*. Then maybe teachers in shacks will quit having winter days when they burn from the waist up and freeze from the waist down.

Television Trauma

An irritation that may be peculiar to our district is that all teachers have been required to watch a telecast from the downtown administration at regular intervals. With the recent advent of a new regime, teachers always hope telecasts may be less frequent. If one of our former superintendents could have sat in a faculty meeting anonymously just once and heard the comments that were made during his presentation, we would probably not have been required to watch any more of his performances.

EVALUATIONS

A baffling facet of teaching 20 or more years ago was that nobody knew what I was doing in my classroom. When I was new to the school system, I used to wonder how the district could have such blind faith in a stranger like me, trusting me for an hour a day with more than 150 young minds. I could have been telling those kids anything. Who checked?

In those days, new teachers were visited on an erratic basis one or two times a year by the district's English chairman as she could find the time. These were 15- or 20-minute visits, and we were warned ahead of time. After the probationary 3 years, teachers were visited only once every 3 years. Considering that lesson plans were required to be produced only if the teacher was absent, one can see that anything might have been going on in the classroom.

I've heard of teachers who kept television sets in their rooms so they wouldn't miss their favorite soap operas. I've walked into classrooms where the entire week's assignments were on the board. Students worked away silently while the teacher read, did needlework, or polished fingernails. Gossip said that classrooms like that were silent not just part of the time, but every day, week after week.

All kinds of efforts have been made in recent years to rid the school system of these nonteaching teachers. Having departmental finals helps if those finals are updated periodically and if teachers who give them don't allow students to delete too many sections of the final. Testing teachers helps, too. However, the tests need to be relevant. Having scored 100% on the math portion of our district's teacher test, I can afford to say that I see no earthly reason why an English teacher should have to pass a math test in order to keep on teaching English. (I consider that 100% a direct miracle. I'd long ago forgotten everything about math except the number facts, and could be argued out of those quite easily.)

Requiring lesson plans to be filed regularly is another effort to make sure teachers are doing what they're supposed to in the classroom. Time consuming and irritating as the plan forms are, I believe most experienced teachers will admit that some kind of commitment in writing should be required of each teacher for each class. It is the only way to ensure that all teachers sit down and think in advance about what they are going to do in their classes in the immediate future, how long it is going to take, what they will need to get it done, and what their purposes are.

Our district some time ago adopted guidelines that require every teacher to be evaluated each semester by two different administrators. A result of this dictum is that all our assistant principals are hideously overburdened and stressed for time. What suffers most is their handling of serious disciplinary situations. Each classroom visit by an AP is now supposed to last 50 minutes or longer.

The visiting administrator brings with him a check sheet on which he rates the teacher's performance. It is loaded with over 70 items. These are divided into five "domains," four of which deal with classroom performance. The fifth is concerned with a teacher's "Growth and Responsibilities" outside the classroom. Not counting the 16 items in Domain V, the assessor is expected to rate the teacher on over 50 items in his 50-minute visit.

It is a comfort to realize that the administrator probably regrets the necessity of his visit as much as or more than the teacher does. Many of the assessors are hoping to find good teaching and learning going on. It helps to remember that.

Having an adult visitor in the classroom made me nervous, no matter how many kids I had taught for how many years. I found it best not to look at the visitor and to try to forget his or her presence entirely. Most kids in most classes will be on their best behavior when an administrator is present. You don't have to warn them. In fact, a good many of the kids somehow get the impression that it is they who are being evaluated. I never considered it necessary to correct that notion.

A habit I developed over the years was to put a do today list on the board to keep the kids and me on track. I have mentioned this in a previous section. It's a very good thing to have visible when you are being evaluated. There are items on the assessor's checklist about defining goals and explaining the importance of class activities to the students. Having that do today list on the board goes a long way toward covering such items.

After the visit, each evaluator is supposed to offer the visited teacher a conference if she wants one. If there are more low marks on your evaluation than you believe are justified, you should indeed request a conference. Most administrators are prepared to be reasonable as to changing low marks if your defense is valid. Perhaps there was a genuine misunderstanding of something that happened during the visit. A little explanation may change a 3 to a 4. A teacher can learn a lot, too, if the visitor points out some weaknesses and explains how to do things better. It's not likely to be fun, but such a conference can be well worth your time.

It's the practice in our district for evaluators always to warn teachers in advance of their visits. However, they may well drop in on your classroom unannounced just because they're nearby, or because you're making more noise than they think is right, or because they are on some entirely different errand. The only safe thing to do is to make sure that all your classroom time is spent doing what you're supposed to be doing. Then you're always ready for company.

TRANSFERRING

The best thing that can happen for a teacher is that she should find a school she likes, settle there, and never leave. Because we as well as our environment are constantly changing, however, it is likely the time will come when you want to transfer from one school to another. Our large district is the only one I can speak for with respect to transfers. Our practice is rather different from our written policy.

I transferred twice in 29 years. Once was from junior high to high school. The other transfer was from that high school to another. In both cases I began by locating the school where I wanted to go, making an interview appointment with its principal, and making certain that I was wanted there.

If a transfer takes place during the school year, one must have the approval of the principal one is leaving. If the transfer is done in summer, the former principal's assent is not needed. My transfer to senior high was a summer one. All I had to do after the interview was to go to my new school on the first day of the fall semester. The opportunity to transfer between high schools came about when my receiving principal had an unexpected opening in the fall. I asked to leave that September, but my principal said to wait until midterm. Luckily for me, the opening still existed in January, and I reported to the new school on the in-service day between semesters.

I hesitated a long time before each of those two moves, and I would advise any teacher to do likewise. I never regretted either move, and that's what it took so long to make sure about. Pulling up roots is no fun, and it doesn't get easier as time goes by and friendships deepen. There were people at both the schools I left whom I truly love and miss.

Written district policy, I believe, advises a transferring teacher to consult her present principal first, and then go through the personnel office to find out what is available. Don't you believe it. In our district, you could land at a school that would cost you an hour's ride each way, and that's on our notorious freeways. You need to find out all you can about a school before you even think of going there. If it is not a better situation for you than the one you already have, will it really be worth the upheaval in your life?

Secrecy should be maintained in the early stages of working on a transfer. The best thing you can tell your friends about what you are doing is nothing. They will forgive you when they know why. It is only human nature for a principal to feel some resentment for a teacher who wants to leave his school. And then, to be practical, would he be wise to give one of his better assignments to a person who, if stopped from leaving during the school year, might leave during the following summer?

ADMINISTRATIONESE

A special language emanates from our central school district administration—Downtown, as the teachers in our district call it. I don't know if this is a peculiarity of our district or if there is some basic ingredient in school administration that causes linguistic aberrations. What I have noticed is that in any given year, a majority of the people who work in the administration building adopt certain favorite words and phrases that one just doesn't hear in the population at large. Later, as those words and phrases make their way into areas other than education, the educators come up with new favorite expressions.

For instance, we have heard "contact" used a verb for so long now, it has almost lost its sting. New verbs in use by the folks Downtown are "conference" ("Are you going to conference him today?" "We are conferencing with the principals on this") and "impact" ("We expect this to impact our social studies department." "How will this news impact the new teachers?"). A favorite of mine is "service." Almost every time a certain administrator from Downtown spoke to a teacher group, we heard how he wanted to service us. In the farm and ranch county where I grew up, service is what a bull does for a cow. Makes one downright nostalgic to hear the old expression again.

Nobody Downtown ever just tells you anything any more, they "share" it with you. Expect to hear yourself being thanked often for sharing tidbits with them, even if you had no such generosity in mind. Good, bad, or indifferent, all our utterances nowadays are pieces of pie to be endlessly, graciously handed out to whoever is listening. Then the listener, of course, shares his response with you.

There is nothing grammatically wrong with it, but I get a little edgy when a speaker starts using the phrases "these kinds of things" or "those kinds of things" a bit too often. It sounds to me somewhat self-consciously strained. Surely sometimes it would be in order to say simply, "these things" or "those things." A lot of Downtown speakers sprinkle "kinds of things" through their remarks so plentifully as to be distracting.

A major enterprise with Downtown people nowadays is "identifying the problem." I get the impression that hours, days, and weeks are spent identifying problems that any teacher could have identified for them in about 10 minutes' time. They do not seem to feel the need of teachers' help, though. In my whole teaching career I was never asked to help any administrator identify any problem. The closest I came was filling out one of those multipage surveys wherein both the questions and the answers are loaded. You get to choose among "sometimes," "never," "always," and the like—those kinds of things.

After they get the problem identified, what do these highly paid, higher level administrators do? Why, they address it, of course. "Now see here, Problem—" This is also known as "speaking to" the problem. What they never seem to get around to is solving some of them.

Recently, the people Downtown have taken up "interfacing." Like the tango, it takes two to interface. As I understand it, two administrators may interface—in old-fashioned terms, work together or pool resources—or two departments may interface, or two projects may interface. I have also heard something said about concepts or concerns interfacing. *That* is not a situation I want to inquire about more deeply.

Of course, "prioritizing" has been going on in our district for years. It's hard to say whether this new verb originated with educators or with government bureaucrats. Whichever, it is another handy thing one can do with problems—I suppose, after they have been identified and addressed—in lieu of having to get down to solving them.

It is perfectly possible in a large school district to teach 20 or 30 years and to avoid all contact with the administrators Downtown. That is what I would advise any new teacher to do. Just make sure your name is down there in the payroll department and your personnel records are in order, and you won't need to make any other contact with the Downtown people except for what you may read about them in the news media. Unless you're trying to transfer or perhaps to join them, they don't have anything else you need Downtown.

If you insist on carrying a problem or a gripe Downtown, for heaven's sake, remember to call it a "concern." That is a highly respectable thing to have, and any administrator in his right mind knows he'd better take an interest in your concerns. Being mad or irritated or just plain outraged could get you labeled a troublemaker who needs to be transferred to the boondocks, but you've got the moral drop on them the minute you are concerned. And, of course, what you do with a concern is to share it! Then the administration owes you thanks for sharing your concern. It is then their move to address your concern or to speak to it.

I don't suppose any school district the size of ours could have a Downtown that did not draw heavy criticism from the faculties in the various buildings. We ought to remind ourselves that there are some things our district does right. Still, it seems to me that serious consideration ought to be given to the idea that there is an optimum size for a school district. When that size is surpassed, there is likely to be a deadening loss of contact between the individual teacher and the administrators who, after all, are there only to see that her job gets done in the most effective possible way.

If the supervisors of every academic department were to die overnight and we teachers didn't read about it in the paper or see it on television, what difference would it make to our jobs and the way we do them? I hope somebody Downtown is developing concern about that question and identifying the problem.

10

ENDING AND
BEGINNING

GETTING THE BUSINESS FROM BUSINESS

Some years ago I prepared an in-service presentation on teaching poetry in junior high. Before my 2-hour session began, there was a general assembly of the English teachers across the district. We were addressed by a businessman, a rather important CEO. He gave us a number of horror stories about the grammatical and syntactical inadequacies of people who applied for jobs with his company.

He was letting us know, albeit politely, just what a lousy job we were doing in getting the basics of language usage across to our students and what a hardship that worked for him when he came to need competent new employees. I could not have agreed with him more. Where he and I differed was in placing the blame. That man sincerely believed the problem was 100% the fault of inadequate teachers. I beg to differ.

Nobody stood up and told that CEO that he and businessmen like him needed to accept a hefty share of responsibility for the poorly spoken, ungrammatical Americans one encounters everywhere today, but a lot of us teachers wanted to do just that. I delayed the start of my poetry session because I simply had to blow off steam to my audience of English teachers about the unfair hit we had all just taken.

Businessmen sponsor television and radio programs. Those programs present speakers who butcher the language unmercifully.

Sometimes the producers tolerate such lapses because the speakers are "personalities" and their sayings are "cute." Peggy Cass, for example, started half the country saying, "I could care less" when they mean the opposite, "I couldn't care less." At the time, Peggy Cass was cute. A lot of people wanted to sound like her.

Mission Impossible butchered the verb "destroy" into "destruct"— "this tape will self-destruct . . ." It is almost impossible for students in an American classroom to be convinced that destruct is just a piece of the noun *destruction.*

Winston cigarettes substituted the preposition *like* for the subordinating conjunction *as.* Now we have clauses that are virtually folk sayings, such as "tell it like it is." I've read that the Winston cigarette people, advised early and often that there was wrong grammar in their ads, commented, "They noticed! That's great!" Did their CEOs sing a different tune when they wanted to hire people who were at least semiliterate?

Howard Pools put up billboards all over our city showing the nether half of a female figure in a bathing suit. Her top half appeared to be under water. The message? "She just *dove* into a Howard Pool." I'm told that, advised of the fact that dived is the past tense of dive, the advertisers for that company reacted the same way the Winston people did.

What the CEOs do not seem to understand is that they cannot have it both ways. They cannot actively promote bad usage in order to sell their products and then turn on and revile the teachers who try to combat the incessant drumbeat of ignorance and conscious, arrogant misuse of our language. Put your money where your mouths are, fellows. You want good grammar? Write ads that use good grammar. Insist on hiring performers who use good grammar at least most of the time. Don't make wrong usage look attractive or excuse it with "everybody says it this way."

In the sciences, in social studies, in the arts, as well as in languages, schools used to be the major sources of information young people received. It isn't that way any more. Everyone who uses mass communication in any form needs to take responsibility for seeing that his or her message comes through with facts reliable and language accurate. With respect to daily use of the language, there is no longer any way the schoolroom can compete with the tube.

That is what I told the teachers at my session, and what I would have liked to tell that CEO, if he hadn't been an invited guest. Anyway, the teachers knew exactly what I was talking about. It was more truth than poetry.

BEING PROFESSIONAL

Every time an administrator starts talking about how "professional" you are, get worried. Often such talk is a preface to asking you to donate free time to such enterprises as monitoring students at football games or guarding the candy line in the cafeteria. Sometimes your being a professional is supposed to prevent you from complaining when you read that garbage collectors in New York City make more than you do. It is also a reminder that professionals don't strike to better their working conditions.

While we are talking about what professionals do not do, here is a short list of my own.

Real professionals should not

1. have to order books and workbooks to be issued to their clientele and stand personally responsible financially for such materials;
2. have to do guard duty in cafeterias, halls, and restrooms in addition to teaching a full load of students;
3. have to teach a "tutorial" of 35 extra minutes or more daily in addition to the regular teaching load, without receiving a penny in compensation;
4. lug home 2 or 3 hours' work *per night* during the week, and more than that on most weekends and holidays;
5. have to keep track of absences and tardies of their clientele and reteach as they may need it;
6. take 30 minutes or fewer (portal to portal) daily for lunch;
7. give whatever additional time is needed before and after business hours for makeups and extra help;

8. call and receive calls from parents after school hours because parents cannot be reached during the business day.

Is teaching a profession? Is it an art? Is it a craft? It is, surely, a "practice" like the practice of medicine or law. After a lifetime of practicing, one can look back and see improvement, but one can never look forward and anticipate perfection.

I believe a teacher is a professional, whatever that means, and ought to be treated like one. I believe more teachers would be more professional if the eight kinds of burdens listed above were removed for good. It could happen if enough people wanted teachers to operate on a level they could truly respect, as lawyers and doctors do.

FALL FEVER

One fall at the filling station, the owner and some of the attendants began teasing me about having to start back to school in a few days. Then they began to remind each other about getting ready to start back in their elementary days—what kinds of lunch kits they carried, Big Chief tablets, pencils, paste, the smell of new school supplies—they never even noticed when I left, they were having such a good time remembering.

Later that day, a friend called to say goodbye before she went back to college to begin her sophomore year. I heard the same excitement in her voice. After I hung up, I wondered how much of that excitement was hers and how much was my own.

After teaching many years, I still got stirred up at the beginning of school each fall. In a few days, we'd be starting everything again. I'd have a potted plant ready to put on that bare spot on the filing cabinet. We'd have 4 days' in-service, then a weekend, then the Labor Day holiday, and we met the kids for the first time on Tuesday. I knew I wouldn't sleep Monday night. It's always like that in September. This year it was always going to be wonderful. This year, I was going to reach them all.

ABOUT THE AUTHOR

Geneva Fulgham graduated as valedictorian of her senior class in Angleton, Texas; earned a bachelor's degree in journalism from Sam Houston State University in Huntsville, Texas; and received an MLA at St. John's Graduate Institute in Santa Fe, New Mexico. She worked as editor of a weekly newspaper, continuity writer for a radio station, bank secretary, and legal secretary before becoming a full-time teacher of English and journalism. She taught for 29 years before retiring to help in family concerns and write poetry and prose. Her mystery *The Murder Sonata* was published under her pen name, Frances Fletcher. She coauthored *Women Pioneers in Texas Medicine* with her sister, Elizabeth Silverthorne, of Salado, Texas. A variety of her poems, short stories, and articles have been published, and a one-act play, *The Principal Thing*, was produced. She is the widow of Henry C. Fulgham, a symphony percussionist and jazz drummer. She lives in Bellaire, an independent suburb of Houston, Texas. Their two children, Mary and Joel, are professional musicians and live nearby.